RACING IN ART

RACING IN ART

JOHN FAIRLEY

RIZZOLI
NEW YORK

First published in the United States of America in 1990 by
Rizzoli International Publications, Inc.
300 Park Avenue South, New York, NY 10010

Library of Congress Cataloging-in-Publication Data

Fairley, John, 1940—
    Racing in art / John Fairley.
        p.   cm.
    ISBN 0-8478-1234-0
    1. Race horses in art. 2. Painting. Modern. I. Title
ND1380.F35   1990
758.3--dc20   90-31401
                                 CIP

Printed in Great Britain
by Richard Clay Ltd, Bungay, Suffolk

Contents

Preface

It is the intention of this book to try to share the delight of racing art — of paintings which have given so much private pleasure and inspiration for the last two and a half centuries, yet by their very nature as items of individual history, have largely been hidden from the general public.

Today, with the generous gifts of Paul Mellon to Yale, the Virginia Museum, the Tate Gallery and elsewhere, some fine paintings have emerged. Lord Vestey's endowment of the gallery at Newmarket has provided, with various exhibitions, a changing glimpse of the glories in private collections. But in some areas the display of sporting art has diminished. The new and refurbished racing museums at Saratoga in New York State and Louisville, Kentucky, offer imaginative and enticing narratives of racing, but they have effectively reduced the space and opportunity to view their racing pictures. The Woodward Collection in Baltimore is also sadly confined. Great pictures surface tantalisingly in the sale rooms of the London and New York auction houses, and then briefly again in the galleries of Bond Street and Park Avenue, only to disappear until another and possibly less enthusiastic generation seeks to market them again.

Racing art has never been designed for or cherished by public galleries. Yet it is perhaps not an exaggeration to suggest that these paintings offer a canvas of character, history, courage, and endeavour comparable to the record of military and maritime painters like Lady Butler or Charles Napier Hemy which are so prominent in our civic rooms, or to the genre painters whose works are so widely on view. Ben Marshall brought a huge talent and a Hogarthian joy to racing painting, yet his works are on show in less than a dozen British public galleries, only two of them within a hundred miles of London. James Pollard may be represented in London — at the Tate and the British Museum — but his work is hardly to be found at all outside the capital.

Several major collections of equestrian art were put together in the last century, only too frequently to be dispersed again. Walter Hutchinson, the publisher, was beggared by his acquisition of nearly three thousand pictures and his foundation of the short-lived

National Gallery of Sports and Pastimes. His collection ended on the auction rostrum of Christie's. Sir Abe Bailey's collection went to the National Gallery of South Africa. Some of Walter Stone's pictures have resurfaced at the Walker Art Gallery in Liverpool after half a century in the vaults.

Racing occupies a special and important niche in art. Its colour, intensity, and variety attracted the talents of some of Europe's most important painters, from Géricault to Manet and Toulouse-Lautrec, even Gauguin. In the last century, Degas became fascinated with Eadweard Muybridge's photographs of animals, and especially horses, in motion. Since then racing has offered to many notable artists the challenge of portraying that glorious, dynamic impression of movement which photography cannot really convey — a challenge perhaps as interesting and profound as the Impressionists' attempt to convey the true impact of light and colour. There are paintings in this book which reveal that, at its best, racing art has attained a quality which transcends the sport that inspired it.

Trotting at the Union Raceway HENRI DELATTRE

Introduction

The evolution of the thoroughbred racehorse came about quite suddenly in England. Within the space of one generation, a breed of animal emerged which had a grace and power quite beyond the capacities of the old horses, the English hobbies, which had provided sport and racing for the men of the seventeenth century.

Today all the thoroughbreds in the world can be traced back to just three Arab stallions imported to England across the turn of the eighteenth century: the Byerley Turk, whom Captain Byerley rode at the Battle of the Boyne (and indeed escaped on); the Godolphin Arabian; and the Darley Arabian. When horsemen realised that the crossing of an Arab or Barb with the English horse could infuse speed and stamina beyond the wildest imagination, expeditions were sent to the heart of Arabia, an enterprise entailing a daunting degree of courage and expense in the early eighteenth century, in order to seek out and purchase the finest stallions. The desert sheiks were not always cooperative. But when a horse like Edward Darley's Arabian survived the long sea journey to be safely installed in the strange green paddocks of England, the effect was outstanding. The awe in which his son Flying Childers was held echoes down the centuries — 'the fleetest horse who ever lived'.

There was an urge, from the beginning, to immortalise these creatures and their exploits on canvas. Many of the early Arabians were painted in idolatrous splendour as a memorial to the exploits of their progeny. And racing became a passion. Throughout the eighteenth century, more and more meetings became established, and the walls of a gentleman's home were as likely to be adorned with pictures of his racers and their triumphs as by portraits of his wife or his ancestors. This obsession was a profitable one for painters, and the century saw the first great flowering of equestrian art in the hands of Stubbs, Seymour, Wootton, and Gilpin.

These pictures were ikons to their owners and have remained so to this day. Wootton's pictures are a principal adornment of Longleat and Landseer's *Voltigeur* of Aske in Yorkshire. Succeeding generations have continued to appreciate them, and the high

The Bloody-Shouldered
Arabian
JOHN WOOTTON

prices which racing art commands in the sale rooms of New York and London today are not just a reflection of artistic merit, but encompass other values redolent of tradition and history.

A monumental painting like that by John Frederick Herring (1795–1865) and James Pollard (1792–1867) of the Doncaster Cup of 1838 is impressive not only for its fascinating crowds and the magnificence of the four classic thoroughbreds galloping across the six-foot canvas, but also for its history, which demonstrates the confluence of taste, money and interest which combine together uniquely in racing art. This great painting was commissioned by the sixth Earl of Chesterfield at a time when Herring alone was charging more than £150 for one of his smaller pictures. It has been cherished by a succession of sportsmen, most recently by H. J. Joel, whose family had made their own contribution to the history of racing since returning to England with South African wealth in the time of Cecil Rhodes. They won the Derby with Sunstar in 1911, Pommern in 1915 and Humorist in 1927. H. 'Jim' Joel won with Royal Palace in 1967, and in 1989, when he was in his nineties, still had a live Derby hope in High Estate. Two years previously he had won the Grand National with Maori Venture.

Racing art offers the exhilaration of looking at a beautiful thoroughbred, the memory of ambition achieved and triumphs savoured. It inspires the same pride as a family portrait. These paintings are a matter of record, of the owner's own part in and connection with the flow of history, with moments of heritage.

Nor are their patrons mere connoisseurs of oils. They have refined their judgement of horse flesh over the years, and backed that judgement with guineas and dollars. They have finely tuned sensibilities for the points of the thoroughbred, whether standing in the stud yard or painted on canvas. These pictures are, of course, the finest decoration in a horseman's home, but conversation pieces too, memorials of shared experience.

Pollard and Herring's picture distils the fine and varied emotions which sustain the patron and connoisseur of racing art. Clearly it was a great day, this Thursday 20 September 1838. The imposing splendour of Doncaster's great four-tier stand, the members' stand, even the judge's box, are all crowded to overflowing. The uniformed stewards are busy turning back the youths who are trying to slip under the rails. Some spectators have come in their hackneys and carriages, notably the four greys on whom

Pollard, so meticulous in these matters, precisely set the details of the tack and traces.

The picture is an enduring reminder for the Earl of Chesterfield of the great press of people who were there to see the finest horse His Lordship ever owned. Don John was awesomely tough; as a two-year-old, he twice defeated The Fairy Queen owned by the fiercest competitor of the time, Squire Osbaldeston. He came to Doncaster for St Leger week as the hot favourite. Not for a moment did he give Chesterfield any anxiety in the classic, winning by twelve lengths in record time, despite being left at the start. Two days later the Earl turned him out again for this Doncaster Gold Cup which he won easily from Beeswing, with the black horse, The Doctor, third and Melbourne fourth.

Chesterfield, with remarkable sang-froid, had also left Don John in the Gascoigne Stakes, one of five horses who were subscribed on the very same afternoon. Fortunately the other four declined the contest and Don John escaped another excursion round the St Leger course, by walking over. He thus collected nearly £4,000 in winnings in two days, and earned his immortality on canvas. For his owner never won another St Leger and never won the Derby, though that same year he won the Oaks with Industry and eleven years later took it again with Lady Evelyn.

The Earl of Chesterfield inherited the title when he was ten years old. When he reached the age of twenty-one he discovered that a large fortune had accumulated, unencumbered, happily, by the sort of clause that his grandfather had put in his will: 'If he should at any time keep any racehorses, or reside one night at Newmarket (that famous seminary of iniquity and ill manners) during the course of the races there . . . he shall forfeit and pay the sum of £5,000 to and for the use of the Dean and Chapter of Westminster.' The sixth Earl set about spending treasure on more earthly pursuits. He indulged in the 'iniquity' of racing, became Queen Victoria's Master of the Royal Buckhounds, and patronised the arts.

Chesterfield was a substantial figure in every sense. A Belvoir Hunt ballad sang of him:

Previous page
Don John Winning the 1838
Doncaster Gold Cup
JOHN FREDERICK HERRING
and JAMES POLLARD

> Who sits his horse so well? Or at a race
> Drives four-in-hand with greater skill or grace?
> And when hounds really run, like him can show
> How fifteen stone should o'er a country go.

14

Beeswing Winning the 1842 Ascot Gold Cup JOHN DALBY

Yet he lives in history most vividly, perhaps, through one great horse, and the splendid and grandiose canvas which immortalised its exploits.

Beeswing, the mare from Northumberland who came second in the Cup, ran on the Turf for eight years, winning fifty-one of her sixty-four races. Pubs and hostelries in Northumberland and Yorkshire are named after her to this day, and she was the subject of numbers of paintings, many of which were turned into prints.

John Dalby of York (*fl.* 1838–53) painted her winning the Ascot Cup of 1842 'cleverly', as the racing jargon goes. The dark bay at the back was the favourite, Lanercost, who in the malevolent custom of the day had, it seems, been poisoned by the betting fraternity.

I
The Era of Idolatry

Thomas Spencer's adulatory picture of the Duke of Bolton's horse Starling is the most powerful example of the veneration which had grown up, within a generation, for the thoroughbred horse. The horse towers over mere men as though he has been sent down from the clouds above by the Gods themselves. The great arching crest dwarfs the grooms beneath, the flashing eye is disdainful. The jockey approaches respectfully, as at the commencement of some sacrament; the groom stands at his head like an altar boy before the ceremony.

Starling at Newmarket THOMAS SPENCER

The picture was painted after the race in 1734 depicted in the background, in which Starling beat Surly Slouch owned by Mr Fry, and Miss Hackney owned by Mr Vane. Miss Hackney is nearly distanced as she passes the running gap on Newmarket Heath, with Starling already almost at the post. It is a picture full of idolatrous sentiment, and was part of the extraordinary record kept by early horsemen of the line, purity and achievements of those animals to whom they afforded such admiration.

Though it is getting on for three centuries now since Starling was foaled — 1727, said the first edition of *The General Stud Book*, and not 1726, as it says on the picture — his history and prowess, like that of nearly all the early racehorses, is known in the most vivid detail. His story epitomises the intense and devoted care initiated in the eighteenth century, and continued to this day, by which the antecedents of every thoroughbred in the world are traceable in almost total detail back three hundred years.

Starling was the son of Bay Bolton. *The Stud Book*, first published in 1791, records: 'Bay Bolton was a good runner, and proved an excellent stallion.' He was bred by Sir Matthew Pierson in 1705. His sire was Grey Hautboy, who, in turn, was a son of Hautboy, bred of D'Arcy's White Turk and a royal mare. The biblical litany is recorded on Bay Bolton's dam's side back to the Oglethorpe Arabian, and on Starling's dam's side to the Brownlow Turk, Pulleine's Chestnut Arabian, and a daughter of the Helmsley Turk. D'Arcy's White Turk was one of the horses imported by Lord D'Arcy — there was a D'Arcy's Yellow Turk as well — some time after the Restoration of Charles II.

There is a contemporary description of the arrival in London of some of the Arabs captured at the siege of Vienna in 1684, when the Poles and the Austrians managed to repel the Turks at the zenith of their assault on Christendom. The King, the Duke of York, and the Prince of Denmark were among the onlookers when the animals were paraded in St James's Park. Five hundred guineas was demanded for one of them: 'so delicate a creature, a bright bay, two white feet, a blaze; such a head, eyes, ears, neck, breast, belly, haunches, legs, pasterns and teeth; in all regards beautiful and proportioned to admiration, spirited, proud, nimble'.

Bay Bolton was a favourite of the Duke, for he twice beat Dragon in matches at Newmarket, and Dragon was the champion of Tregonwell Frampton, the man who first organised racing at Newmarket in regulated fashion, when he was manager of the royal horses from Charles II's time through to that of George II.

When Bay Bolton died at the age of thirty-one he was buried with his shoes on between two stone pillars, the remnants of which are still discernible, at the top of the avenue which ran from Castle Bolton to Middleham High Moor in Wensleydale, Yorkshire.

Starling himself was 'an excellent runner' according to *The Stud Book*. And indeed, thanks to the early annalists like William Pick of York, and Orton, another conscientious Yorkshireman, the fine details of Starling's career are preserved. He raced first at four years old on 13 August 1731, carrying 10 stone, and beat thirteen others for a 20-guinea purse, up at Hambleton on the heights above the Vale of York. The first three were all greys. The Duke took him down to Newmarket the following spring for a hundred-guinea sweepstake, confined to horses which had been the property of their owners for at least two years. Even then, evidently, there was some concern at wealthy upstarts coming in and buying success on the racecourse. Starling won.

The horse now had to walk all the way down to Sussex for Lewes Races at the beginning of August. It was here that the seeds were laid for the match depicted in Spencer's painting, for the horse that Starling defeated in both of the four-mile heats was Surly Slouch. Some peculiarity in the running that day must have convinced Mr Sly that a more profitable tilt at Starling might be envisaged in the future.

A month later Starling was back up at Lincoln to win the King's Plate, and by October he was walking over at Newmarket, the opposition having melted away. The race against Surly Slouch and Miss Hackney for the King's Plate at Newmarket took place on 4 April and the horses finished in the same order in both of the four-mile heats. He was then sold into the stud of Mr Edward Leedes in Yorkshire and died in 1756.

Among his sons were Ancaster's Starling, Teaser, Torrismond and Jason, all by mares sired by Partner — one of the early 'nicks', as successful conjugal affinities are known in racing. Starling was not destined to join the three great Arabians from whose unbroken male line have emerged the thoroughbreds of today. Indeed of the three, Darley's Arabian seems increasingly to be asserting his preeminence in the twentieth century. The last of the Byerley Turk's line to win the Derby at Epsom was Blakeney in 1969, and the last of the Godolphin Arabian's direct descendants to win was Santa Claus in 1964, though his blood through Man o' War is still strong in the United States. Starling's blood, instead, is to be found in thoroughbreds through the female line.

STARLING,
Got by
Bay Bolton, Foald
1727. he Won y four
years Old Plate at
Hambleton, the
Great Stakes, w
four King's
Plates.

Starling with his Cups THOMAS SPENCER

Thomas Spencer (1700–63) painted another picture of Starling, with his plates (which were actually, it seems, cups). This picture, suggesting the rolling downland around Hambleton which was the scene of his first victory, pre-dates the Newmarket painting, for Starling is much darker and has scarcely embarked on that striking whitening process which marks grey horses as they get older and is most graphically shown in Stubbs's different pictures of Gimcrack.

Spencer was originally a portrait and miniature painter, and is known to have been a 'scholar' of James Seymour (1702–52). Seymour was himself the son of a banker who lived in Fleet Street in London. His talents matured early, and his first known painting was dated 1721, when he was nineteen years old. In many cases it would be rash to attribute a painting to one artist or the other, especially as they signed with initials, and sometimes not at all. But it could be claimed that there is a distinctive animation in Spencer's work which is absent in Seymour's graver, more ethereal portraits, as well as a greater concern with the skyscapes and background of his pictures. Spencer and Seymour both contributed to sets of racehorse engravings which were published in the mid eighteenth century.

Along with John Wootton (c.1678–1765), Spencer and Seymour make up the trio of painters to whom we are chiefly indebted not only for the portraits of celebrated horses in that half century of excitement when the fleetness of the new English thoroughbred was making its mark, but also for the atmosphere and feel of racing.

Wootton had studied some of the Dutch and Flemish landscape painters like Claude and Poussin, and worked with Jan Wyck. His picture of a race at Newmarket has the most fulsome sense of space and depth, as well as containing lively and illuminating cameos of the activity on the Heath. The Rubbing Down House, which was the centre of activity and gossip, is already in place, with a cluster of figures round the flagged post nearby where much of the wagering was undertaken — bookmakers, odds and the refinements of gambling being some way in the future. The spire of Newmarket Church and the windmill are in the background. Much of the racing at this time was over two or three four-mile heats, the horses being given about half an hour to be rubbed down and allowed to recover between heats. There is a little group supervising the start as the eight runners set off, the leader already glancing back to make sure the field is not going to make him

Overleaf
Start of a Race at Newmarket
JOHN WOOTTON

21

do all the work. The main crowd however is in the centre, some in carriages, but most already into a canter, ready to follow the runners round the circular course. As racing attracted more followers through the eighteenth century and into the nineteenth, the harum scarum riding of the spectators was to become a genuine hazard both to competitors and to those on foot, until first cords and then railings came into use.

Wootton seems to have been the first man in England to make a career from the painting of racehorses. From this he contrived to live in considerable style with a 'noble

Prince George's Leedes JOHN WOOTTON

painting room' and fees of £40. His clients included King George II, Frederick, Prince of Wales, and many leading racing men.

His portrait of Leedes records a royal transaction. Leedes was a son of the Leedes Arabian who was imported in to Yorkshire by Mr Edward Leedes and appears in the pedigree of Bartlett's Childers as the sire of the grandam, and thus in the line of Eclipse and all his successors. Leedes was bought for one thousand guineas, according to an inscription on the picture, by Queen Anne, and presented to her husband Prince George of Denmark in 1705. Wootton is here setting the style which was to prevail for years to come. The horse, held by a well-turned-out groom, is set against a tasteful landscape and lake with the corner of a stately pile in view. Though this picture was painted to record admiration for the animal, Wootton had no qualms in showing the white marks of old saddle sores on his flanks.

Queen Anne was one of the great royal patrons of racing. Charles II had established the supremacy of Newmarket, with a royal palace there. He had raced — and won — on the Heath in 1671. William III had continued the royal tradition in more sober fashion, though he was a fierce gambler. Anne, who had seen the old Newmarket before the fire of 1683 destroyed much of the town, ordered the rebuilding of the palace and paid frequent visits there. She was also the founder of Royal Ascot, giving the Hundred-guinea Plate, which was the start of racing 'on the new heath at Ascot Common' in 1711.

James Seymour's picture of horses exercising on Newmarket Heath around the 1740s is one of the first illuminations of the elaborate routine which had established itself for the training of racehorses at this early period, and which continues unchanged in many respects to this day. The horses are clearly being exercised as a string, in a disciplined way. Seven are cantering in the distance, while another nine are coming through the gap in the Devil's Dyke to be watered. The grooms have a uniform livery, a last relic of which can be seen on the modern Newmarket Heath where the riders who turn out for morning work sometimes sport stable colours on their skull caps.

Though the picture gives every impression of a warm, even balmy morning, the horses are rugged up under their working saddles with two or three layers of cloths and coats. The practice of working horses in blankets — sweating them heavily with rugs up their necks and over their heads — was to persist well in to the next century, as was the

Newmarket Heath with
Horses Exercising
JAMES SEYMOUR

dreadful custom of bleeding them after they had raced, sometimes with fatal results. The theory was that fitness could be almost entirely equated with the lack of any spare flesh. There is no doubt, however, that the sweating of horses in such a ruthless manner was also associated with perceptions of equine beauty. The slender, lean neck and small head were thought to be desirable features, and were emphasised, even exaggerated, in many sporting paintings, notably by John Ferneley. There is a painting by Charles Towne (1763–1840) from the 1790s which shows a racehorse at full gallop with head and body rugs on. Towne was a coach painter from Wigan in Lancashire who became a landscape painter and then found a clientèle in racing. He returned to Liverpool and became a vice president of the Liverpool Academy.

Thomas Holcroft, the dramatist and friend of William Hazlitt, has given a vivid description of life at Newmarket in the 1750s. He was the son of a poor itinerant shoemaker whose father had filled his head with accounts of race meetings: 'The amazing cunning of sharpers, the cries of the betting chair, the multitude of gaming and drinking booths.' Father and son were at Nottingham when race time came around. Ten days or a fortnight before the races, straggling horses for the different plates began to drop in. Holcroft, who was only thirteen, was fascinated by the rituals of feeding and caring for the racehorses and also by how prosperous the grooms seemed in their livery. He accordingly persuaded his father to find him a place in a Newmarket stable. There were evidently already a number of well-established stables in the town and he finally became employed by John Watson.

Holcroft has left us a description of stable life two and a half centuries ago, much of which — apart from the extremely early start — will be familiar to lads today.

All the boys at the stable rise at the same hour, from half-past two in spring, to between four and five in the depth of winter. The horses hear them when they awaken each other, and neigh, to denote their eagerness to be fed. Being dressed, the boy begins with carefully clearing out the manger, and giving a feed of oats, which he is obliged no less carefully to sift. He then proceeds to dress the litter; that is, to shake the bed on which the horse has been lying, remove whatever is set or unclean and keep the remaining straw in the stable for another time. The whole stables are then thoroughly

Opposite
Racehorse Galloping with
Jockey Up
CHARLES TOWNE

swept, the few places for fresh air are kept open, the heat of the stable gradually cooled, and the horse, having ended his first feed, is roughly cleaned and dressed. In about half an hour after they begin, or a little better, the horses have been rubbed down, and reclothed, saddled, each turned in his stall, then bridled, mounted and the whole string goes out for the morning exercise; he that leads being the first, for each boy knows his place.

Except by accident, the racehorse never trots. He must either walk or gallop; and in exercise, even when it is the hardest, the gallop begins slowly and gradually, and increases till the horse is nearly at full speed. When he has galloped half-a-mile, the boy begins to push him forward, without relaxation, for another half-mile. This is at the period when the horses are in full exercise, to which they come by degrees. The boy that can best regulate these degrees among those of light weight, is generally chosen to lead the gallop; that is he goes first out of the stable, and first returns.

In the time of long exercise comes the first brushing gallop. A brushing gallop signifies that the horses are nearly at full speed before it is over, and it is commonly made at last rather up hill. Having all pulled up, the horses stand some two or three minutes and recover their wind; they then leisurely descend the hill and take a long walk; after which they are brought to water. But in this, as in everything else (at least as soon as long exercise begins), everything given to them is measured. The boy counts the number of times the horse swallows when he drinks, and allows him to take no more gulps than the groom orders, the fewest in the hardest exercise, and one horse more or less than another, according to the judgement of the groom. After watering, a gentle gallop is taken, and after that, another walk of considerable length; to which succeeds the second and last brushing gallop, which is by far the most severe. When it is over, another pause, thoroughly to recover their wind, is allowed them, their last walk is begun, the limits of which are prescribed, and it ends in directing their ride homewards.

The morning's exercise often extends to four hours, and the evening's to much about the same time. Being once in the stable, each lad begins his labour. He leads the horse into his stall, ties him up, rubs down his legs with straw, takes off his saddle and body clothes; curries him carefully; then, with both curry-comb and brush, never

Eclipse
GEORGE STUBBS

leaves him till he has thoroughly cleaned his skin, so that neither spot nor wet, nor any appearance of neglect, may be seen about him. The horse is then reclothed, and suffered to repose for some time, which is first employed in gratifying his hunger, and recovering his weariness. All this is performed, and the stables are once more shut up, about nine o'clock.

A total eclipse of the sun is an ineffable event. The earth goes dark quite suddenly and an awed silence descends. Birds stop singing. In the cathedral-like hush, all movement seems to stop for two or three minutes, until with a flash like a diamond, the first rim of the sun emerges from behind the moon like some celestial sign of life reborn. It was during these sublime moments of the eclipse in 1764 that the greatest racehorse that ever lived was born. He was, of course, named Eclipse.

His life was to coincide with the most productive period of England's greatest equestrian artist, George Stubbs (1724–1806). Stubbs painted the study of Eclipse on p. 31 when the horse was about six years old. The contrast with paintings that had come before is startling. The horse pushing his head out towards the approaching jockey is entirely naturalistic. There is none of the stylised formality which marks Wootton's work, or that of Spencer or Seymour. This must be how Eclipse really looked, long-bodied, with powerful quarters and good sloping shoulders, though not a big horse. Stubbs gives the chestnut coat a splendid lifelike sheen. To owners who assessed their animals with the most scrupulous eye, Stubbs's pictures must have represented an entirely new level of accomplishment.

Eclipse had been bred by George III's brother, the Duke of Cumberland, but on the Duke's death in 1765 he was purchased by William Wildman, a Smithfield dealer. By the time he first raced he had already attracted the attention of Colonel Dennis O'Kelly who was to buy first a share in and then all of Eclipse, and thereby accumulate a fortune in stud fees, as Eclipse proved to be one of the most influential stallions in the history of the thoroughbred.

When Eclipse first raced at Epsom in 1769, O'Kelly had laid out considerable sums on his success; such was his confidence indeed that he also offered even money or better that he could predict the outcome of the race, including the order of finish of the five horses as they would be posted after the race. 'When called on to declare,' the annals report, 'he said, Eclipse first and the rest in no place.' During the race the horses were all together until the three-mile post, when John Oakley, Eclipse's jockey, flourished the whip. Eclipse set off at such a pace that even though Oakley was hauling on his mouth for the last mile he distanced the others so far that they were not awarded a place at all — and O'Kelly won his wager.

Stubbs was born in Liverpool and became, initially, a portrait painter. But after studying medical anatomy in order to illustrate a surgeon's book on midwifery, he then embarked on the most rigorous programme of training that can be imagined. He took himself off, with his wife Mary Spencer, into reclusive retreat in Lincolnshire, in order to analyse the anatomy of the horse. In a remote cottage in Horkstow he hauled in the carcasses of horses and strung them up in order to dissect them and then draw each layer

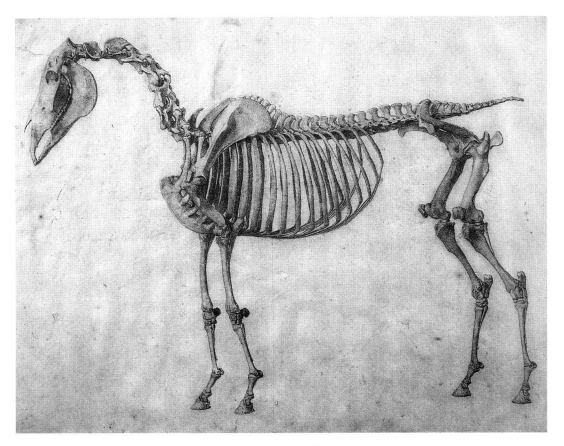

Drawing from *The Anatomy of the Horse* GEORGE STUBBS

of flesh, sinew and bone. The result, published in 1766 as *The Anatomy of the Horse*, is one of the most remarkable products even of that optimistic Age of Enlightenment.

When he emerged from this single-minded sojourn he moved to London, where his talents were quickly recognised by racing men of the time. One of the first pictures he painted was of the Duke of Richmond's horses being exercised at Goodwood, watched by the Duchess and Lady Louisa Lennox. The ordered canter up the hill, disturbed only by the snapping dog, each horse and rider caparisoned in the Richmond yellow, is balanced by the busy scene on the right as the grey horse submits to the attentions of four grooms, after the morning gallop.

33

The Duke of Richmond's
Horses Exercising at
Goodwood
GEORGE STUBBS

Mares and Foals GEORGE STUBBS

Stubbs's classic pictures are the relaxed bucolic friezes of mares and foals, hunters at grass, and thoroughbreds out in the paddocks, often with a lad or groom feeding them. In his mature years he was diverted from the racing scene by other subjects, like the exotic animals that were being imported into England — cheetahs, zebras, monkeys, lions, even a rhinoceros. There is also a series of paintings of a horse being attacked by a lion. He worked in enamel for his friend Josiah Wedgwood. He painted few pictures of racing, but in the 1790s he returned to the subject of the thoroughbred with a series of sixteen portraits of famous horses for the *Turf Review*.

Not all of Stubbs's horse paintings have the animation and emotion of his horse and lion series, but there are some splendidly dramatic pictures, notably the huge canvases of Whistlejacket and Hambletonian. There is also a charming study of Blank, one of the Godolphin Arabian's sons, who was leading sire in 1762, 1764 and 1770. He is shown

Opposite
The Stallion Blank
GEORGE STUBBS

36

Whisker Beating Raphael JOHN NOST SARTORIUS

prancing playfully with his groom in a rustic setting, tail flying and muscles rippling, the groom aquiline and characterful, in calm control.

Blank was as unpromising as his name on the racecourse, and was sold on by his owner, the Earl of Godolphin, before managing to win one minor match. He ended in the hands of one of the major breeders of George III's time, the Duke of Ancaster. He sired twenty-eight winners of forty-two races in his best year, 1764, but it was left to one of the other sons of the Godolphin Arabian, Cade, to provide the male line of descent which has lasted through to the twentieth century.

Stubbs's virtual abandonment of the racing scene for almost twenty years left the field open for some lesser talents, notably the Sartorius family. There were four generations active in horse painting, from John (1700–c.1780), a German immigrant to England in the 1720s, through Francis (1734–1804) to John Nost Sartorius (1759–1828) and his son John Francis (c.1775–1831). They were prodigious in many ways — Francis apparently had five wives — but notably in their output. For fifty years from the 1770s through to John Nost's death in 1828 they chronicled the principal horses and events of the English turf.

John Nost's picture of Whisker and Raphael is typical of the works which were reproduced as prints for a large public. It is a literal visual interpretation of two horses 'stride for stride' at the finish. These were memorial pictures — in this case of the 1815 Derby and the solitary victory in that race of the fourth Duke of Grafton, who won nineteen other classics.

The picture has a naive charm, with the jockeys flourishing their whips and the horses at full stretch, but it makes no pretence to reality. Apart from the eerie absence of any sign of spectators on Epsom Downs, the finish actually involved three horses. The ghost absent from the feast is Busto. He was supposed to be the pacemaker for his owner General Gower's other horse, Raphael; in fact he very nearly won the race. A furlong from home he was in the lead until John Jackson managed to get Raphael past him a few yards from the winning post, only to have Whisker pass him in turn to win by a short head on the line, with Busto only a neck away third. This heart-stopping finale so agitated the public, who had made Raphael the clear favourite, that John Jackson was dragged from the saddle as he rode in and given a beating.

Whisker turned out to be a good stallion: his son Memnon won the 1825 St Leger and another son, The Colonel, the 1828 running; one of his daughters, Emma, was a grandam of the first English triple crown winner, West Australian. Whisker, a full brother of the 1810 Derby winner, Whalebone, was supposed to have an outstanding conformation for a racehorse, though it is difficult to discern it here.

There are numerous portraits of racehorses by John Nost's father, Francis Sartorius, again with a rather primitive appeal. Francis, however, had an eye for comedy and action. He produced an amusing version of one of the odder events on Newmarket Heath, the

Match Between the Barry and the Meynell Hounds FRANCIS SARTORIUS

Alicia Thornton's Match against Captain Flint

match between two couple of hounds, owned respectively by John Smith Barry and Hugo Meynell. Barry's supporters, hats in the air, are shown enjoying the sweetest of victories, in that tradition has here triumphed. Meynell, Master of the Quorn, had started breeding hounds for speed so that they could take a field across the Leicestershire countryside at a pace which entailed thrilling gallops and jumps for the followers, rather than the more sedate pace of generations past. Smith Barry collected £200 from Meynell on this occasion, but it is unlikely he could have repeated the feat much later as the speed of Meynell's hounds became unchallengeable.

Of Stubbs's notable contemporaries, the most able was Sawrey Gilpin (1733–1807), who came from Scaleby in Cumbria. He moved to London and rapidly acquired some aristocratic patrons for whom he painted hunting and equestrian scenes. His most colourful employer was Colonel Thornton whom Gilpin and his son-in-law the artist George Garrard accompanied on his sporting tours of France and Scotland, dealing the most variegated mayhem to the wildlife of those parts, using gun, rod, bow, dog and even baited foxhounds.

Colonel Thornton lived at Thornville Royal near Wetherby and was married — or perhaps not precisely wed — to Alicia, who caused a sensation in 1804 by riding a match against Captain Flint on the Knavesmire course at York. Alicia Thornton was twenty-

A Ladies' Horse Race
THOMAS H. NICHOLSON

two years old when she challenged Captain Flint after a vehement argument in the hunting field over her merits as a horsewoman. She turned out on her husband's horse Vinagrillo wearing a leopardskin jacket with blue cap and riding side-saddle for the four-mile match on 25 August. There was a crowd estimated at a hundred thousand present, many of whom had walked fifty miles from Teesside to see this unique event, and they made Alicia Thornton 6/4 on favourite. For the first three miles she was leading comfortably before Vinagrillo abruptly broke down, and Captain Flint won with ease. It was to be a century and a half before a woman was again allowed to race ride on an English course, though Thomas Henry Nicholson (d.1870) did a furiously exuberant sketch of a ladies' horse race in 1839. Sadly, the event seems to have occurred only in his imagination.

Sawrey Gilpin painted some of the great horses of his day, in particular Highflyer, the stallion who made the fortune of Richard Tattersall. His predeliction, however, was for fiery scenes of snorting thoroughbreds — *Horses Frightened by Lightning* was repeated in several versions — and also of mares and foals at grass. By the time he died, the gracious and exclusive world of aristocratic racing which had sustained Gilpin and Stubbs, Seymour and Spencer, was giving way to the tempestuous era of villainy and chicanery which characterised the early nineteenth century.

Horses Frightened by Lightning SAWREY GILPIN

II
The Cut Throats

Ben Marshall's classic painting of the famous match between Sir Joshua and Filho da Puta on Newmarket Heath in 1816 symbolises the enormous and dramatic social changes which had overtaken racing — and indeed England — with the coming of the turnpike roads, and which were soon to be intensified with the arrival of the railways.

No longer do we see the select and aristocratic contests organised by and for the gentlemen of Yorkshire or the members of the Jockey Club. Racing was becoming accessible to all sorts and conditions of men — and women. And they were to take to it with a relish which ushered in an era of riotous change and excess. Every hold, trick, chicanery or subterfuge that horsemen could devise made its appearance on the Turf. On one of the few occasions when such shifts and devices ended up in court, the judge remarked: 'If gentlemen condescend to race with blackguards, they must condescend to be cheated.' This roistering, colourful, knavish world of rakes, sharpers, and horse copers found the most splendid chronicler in Ben Marshall (1768–1834). It was Marshall who made the famous remark: 'I discover many a man who will pay me fifty guineas for painting his horse, who thinks ten guineas too much to pay for painting his wife.' And indeed his horses are magnificent, muscled, usually a lovely sheen to them, standing out from the canvas, almost in relief.

But it is the character and variety of the spectators and horsemen around them which give his work such quality and interest. Every figure in this picture is individual, from the stony-faced judge in his box, determined, above all, not to be distracted from his duties by the mob around him, to the little girl who has sneaked in front of him, small enough though not to interfere with his line of vision. A diminutive, anxious young swell ushers two small boys back behind the cords and towards the matronly surveillance of the ladies in red.

The roughs and hard men are glimpsed beyond the horses' quarters, supervising the destiny of their wagers. A group of unaccompanied ladies has arrived by carriage and

Sir Joshua Beating Filho da Puta BEN MARSHALL

Sir Joshua and Filho da Puta
at the Start
BEN MARSHALL

secured an excellent view, its most portly member evincing immodest enthusiasm as she waves the contestants home.

The action too is keen, hot-blooded. These two horses are all out, with both jockeys sitting deep into the saddle for the final drive. There is still the 'rocking horse' gallop, so irritating to modern eyes, as there would be for the best part of the century. But this is a far more vigorous, lively and convincing horse race on canvas than anything that had gone before. Stubbs, for sure, could not have matched it, nor Gilpin, nor any of the Sartorius family.

The match that Marshall depicts here, which took place on 15 April 1816, aroused enormous interest, not least because of the stakes involved — 1,000 guineas, ten times the value of the King's Plates which were the centrepiece of many meetings at that time. But there was plenty of other spice to the encounter. Filho da Puta had won the St Leger at Doncaster the year before. According to the *Turf Annals*: 'Immense sums of money were depending upon the event.' Filho da Puta, however, seems to have given his supporters little cause for anxiety on that occasion, for his jockey John Jackson brought him home 'in a common canter'. His owner Sir William Maxwell completed a most satisfactory day at Doncaster by selling him to Mr Houldsworth for 3,000 guineas.

The St Leger, in that era, was easily the most popular race of the year, and it was the ambition of every horseman to topple the victor and make his own horse champion. Keenest of all in that winter of 1815–16 was the Hon. R. Neville. Neville had discovered early in 1815 that he had a really smart colt, when Sir Joshua, who was by Rubens out of a sister to Haphazard, won the Riddlesworth Stakes at Newmarket in April. Mr Neville rather disdained condition races, and had a marked and old-fashioned taste for match racing, one horse against another, no fuzzing of the picture with other contestants, private purse against private purse.

In October 1815 he put Sir Joshua up against Mr Stonehewer's colt Delville for 500 guineas, and won. A couple of weeks later, after allowing the colt to collect a modest 150 guineas in the Oatlands Stakes, he challenged Mr Payne's colt Quinola for 200 guineas, and won again.

The match against Filho da Puta emerged from the winter round of boasting and debate on the merits of thoroughbreds, which rules the thoughts of horsemen to this day.

Mr Houldsworth accepted Neville's challenge for a match at 1,000 guineas. Mr Houldsworth 'jocked off' John Jackson and put up the Yorkshire favourite Thomas Goodison on Filho da Puta. William Arnull rode Sir Joshua.

Marshall's companion picture shows the horses at the start, where, as it transpired, the match was won and lost. Filho reared up as Goodison tried to get him away and lost several lengths. Then coming down the dip towards the bushes on what is now the Rowley Mile, Filho, gaining fast, slipped and was left with too much to make up. Sir Joshua duly won. Flushed with success Mr Neville ran Sir Joshua against Lord Foley's mare Scheherazade, and won another 200 guineas. Nemesis for Mr Neville finally came when he presumed to challenge the 1815 Derby winner Whisker and agreed in a fit of hubris that Sir Joshua should give him six pounds advantage. The Duke of Grafton, Whisker's owner, collected the 300 guineas, and Sir Joshua never raced again.

Marshall can rarely resist including the horsemen in his racehorse portraits, often to the extent that they take over the picture. In his painting of Anticipation and Bourbon, there is an irresistibly comic and appealing group attending the two animals. While the main actors, the two jockeys, are consigned to the shadows of a doorway at the rubbing down house, the eager stable hands bustle about their charges. The midget lads, straining credulity by their size, let alone by their top hats, are in fact probably realistic. It was quite common in the first century of thoroughbred racing for the horses to carry lads weighing less than four stone.

The driving force behind racing's popularity all over the world has been the urge to gamble. But there can have been few epochs when it was as furious, uncontrolled and ruinous as in England in the first half of the nineteenth century. Thomas Rowlandson (1756–1827), most joyous and unfettered of artists, found much inspiration for his ripe and comic cartoons and drawings in the doings at the race track, whether it was the sozzled confusion on the road to Epsom for the Derby, or the hilarious throng, dogs, children, gypsies and all, at a race meeting at York. But, above all, he savoured the gambling. His ink and watercolour *The Betting Post* shows the frenetic mêlée round the mounted layers, as the crowd attempts to get its money on. The fever to lose money has a long history. In this picture the dishevelled military-looking person with the crutches is said to be Colonel O'Kelly and the Prince of Wales is on the left.

Anticipation and Bourbon
BEN MARSHALL

The Road to Epsom THOMAS ROWLANDSON

York Races THOMAS ROWLANDSON

Crockford, the Shark Keeper
of Hell Gaming House,
Piccadilly
THOMAS ROWLANDSON

Previous page
The Betting Post
THOMAS ROWLANDSON

By 1818 Tattersall's establishment at Hyde Park Corner, primarily designed for his twice-weekly horse auctions, had evolved into the centre of gambling in London. James Pollard painted a picture of that weekly appointment with fate, Monday afternoons, settling day at Tattersall's. The subscription rooms are at the back, while the members of the Ring sit at tables paying out or collecting gambling debts. In the main concourse members stroll around taking or laying wagers. It is an insouciant and ordered scene. Here, however, fortunes were gained and tossed away, families broken, lives ruined. 'Amid that hoarse and multifarious miscellany of men, and under exteriors which are at times unpromising,' wrote H. H. Dixon under his pseudonym The Druid in the *Sporting Magazine*, 'are as clear-cutting wits as ever nestled in a brain pan.' The Druid described Scrope Davies, 'who cut his throat regularly after every Newmarket meeting, till the doctors knew exactly when to expect a sewing-up summons', and the debtors scrambling to escape from Doncaster. He saw one meet his creditor and immediately set off for Conisboro Woods with the creditor in pursuit. There he stayed until nightfall, when a friend extracted his carpet bag from his lodgings and they made their escape. 'His pursuer expressed strong fears that both of them would be "roarers" for life, in consequence of the pace up to the Don, where he was driven off.'

The most famous bookmaker, William Crockford, who was one of Rowlandson's subjects, was the centre of a legion of unflattering stories. He certainly bribed the starter and probably the jockey of Mameluke in the 1827 St Leger and then lived to see his own Derby hope Ratan nobbled in 1844. He took sick with shock and died within two days, though it is said that his friends propped the corpse in the window of his house, so that they could collect his Epsom debts.

But the Ring was full of characters, as The Druid listed: 'With Jem Bland, Jerry Cloves, Myers (an ex-butler), Richard (the Leicester stockinger), Mat Milton, Tommy Swan of Bedale (who never took or laid but one bet on a Sunday), Highton, Holliday, Gully, Justice, Crockford, Briscoe, Crutch Robinson, Ridsdale, Frank Richardson and Bob Steward, the art of bookmaking arose, and henceforward, what had been more of a pastime among owners, who would back their horses for a rattler when the humour took them, and not shrink from having £5,000 to £6,000 on a single match, degenerated into a science.'

Settling Day at Tattersalls JAMES POLLARD

Jem Bland made enough to buy a mansion in Piccadilly. His brother had made a fortune farming out the concession to collect tolls on the turnpike. Gully and Ridsdale were partners, and were supposed to have won £50,000 on St Giles's Derby in 1832 and another £35,000 on Margrave's St Leger the same year; such killings could not last and the two fell out. Though Gully prospered, the split was the end for Ridsdale. His high point on the racecourse had been St Giles's victory in his colours in the 1832 Derby.

Ridsdale had been a post boy in York and a butler at Skelton Castle before he took to wagering. He made enough to buy the considerable estate at Murton outside York. But his rift with Gully proved to be not only bitter but ruinous. Gully who, as the ex-champion prize fighter of England, was no man with whom to quarrel, attacked Ridsdale with a whip when they were out hunting. Ridsdale took him to court for assault and York Assizes awarded him £500 in 1834. But by Leger time the next year Ridsdale's luck was gone. On the fateful Monday of settling day Ridsdale was nowhere to be found. Murton, his estates and his stud were sold. It was the end. Ridsdale was eventually to die in penury in a Newmarket stable loft.

Crutch Robinson made his pile leaning against the wall at Newmarket's Betting Rooms and offering odds against the apparently invincible 1834 Derby winner Plenipotentiary, in the St Leger. 'Plenipo' was nobbled so comprehensively before the Doncaster race that he almost died in his stall. The ruthless destruction of horses like Plenipotentiary, for betting reasons, or the bribery of jockeys and officials, became ever more flagrant through the 1830s and 40s. Yet many owners were reluctant to urge action, for they themselves were gambling on a massive scale, while the bookmakers were in turn prominent owners.

Many of J. F. Herring's magisterial portraits of horses are memorials to some of the more villainous aspects of the Turf. He painted two glowing studies of John Gully's pair of classic winners, the filly Mendicant who took the Oaks in 1846 and the colt Pyrrhus the First who won the Derby the same year, though by then Gully was deemed 'a mere fancy bettor now', having made the transition from prize fighting, through bookmaking, to a point where 'as a judge of racing and the points of a horse combined, he has scarcely a peer among his own or the younger generation of turfites'.

Three years earlier Herring had painted the sumptuous tribute to Cotherstone, the

John Gully's Filly Mendicant
JOHN FREDERICK HERRING

John Gully's Colt Pyrrhus
the First
JOHN FREDERICK HERRING

1843 Derby winner, which is now in the Queen Mother's collection. Cotherstone epitomised the explosive alchemy which was racing at the time — brave victories, secret and monumental gambling coups, nobbling, and the start of the drive to clean up racing. The set of pictures shows Cotherstone, with William Scott in the saddle, surrounded by his illustrious forebears: the mystical mingling of blood which produces supremely fast thoroughbreds. There is Cotherstone's sire, Touchstone, then back through the male line, Camel and Whalebone; Cotherstone's dam Emma, and her sire and dam, Whisker and Gibside Fairy.

Cotherstone was bred in the remote fastnesses of Streatlam in the north of England by the extraordinary John Bowes. At the end of a career in which he bred and raced four Derby winners, and owned the first horse to win the Triple Crown, West Australian, Bowes was so little known that his jockey George Fordham had to ask who he was when he was giving out riding instructions. He lived much of his life in Paris, marrying the actress and painter Josephine Coffin-Chevallier. Yet through Cotherstone he was a central figure in the attempt to reform the Turf.

Cotherstone was trained at Malton by William Scott's brother John. One day early in the spring Mr Bowes turned up on the Langton gallops to see his colt tried. By all accounts Bill Scott was so taken aback at the horse's turn of foot that he stopped riding him. But Bowes had seen enough. He forthwith set off for London and backed Cotherstone for the Derby. He stood to win £23,000. This was the year of one of Lord George Bentinck's great 'plunges', when he backed his own horse Gaper to win £135,000 at Epsom, while covering himself on Cotherstone. Cotherstone duly won, though Gaper's trainer John Kent harboured suspicions about the jockey Sam Rogers which were to surface in his memoirs a full fifty years later: 'Rogers rattled Gaper along so mercilessly that the deep ground soon brought him to a standstill.'

When the St Leger came, William Scott was not fit to ride, and Frank Butler was in the saddle. It seems certain that Butler was paid to pull Cotherstone, and he was beaten by the outsider Nutwith. This was the year when Lord George Bentinck was campaigning to make defaulters pay their gambling debts. Some of the recalcitrants struck back by taking out writs against certain big gamblers, as betting was still technically illegal in England, though openly and flagrantly conducted. Bowes found himself with a writ claiming the

Cotherstone and his Forebears JOHN FREDERICK HERRING
with, clockwise from top left, Gibside Fairy, Whalebone,
Camel, Touchstone, Emma, Whisker

John Bowes
J. M. NEGELEN

full amount he was supposed to have won on Cotherstone. He was forced to flee to Paris, while Lord George pursued the matter through Parliament.

The Manly Sports Bill finally became law, repealing the statutes against gambling, in February 1844. Bowes returned to England in time for the infamous Derby of 1844, and with Bentinck and John Scott wrote a seminal letter asking the Epsom stewards to investigate the most notorious stew of malpractice in racing history. The signatories pursued the case to the bitter end, finally revealing that the winner of the three-year-old colt's classic, Running Rein, an alias for Maccabeus, was actually four; that another runner, Leander, was probably six; that the favourite, Ugly Buck, was deliberately knocked out by foul riding and that Crockford's horse Ratan was not only nobbled the night before, but also pulled by Sam Rogers, just in case.

That race marked the nadir of a sport which has always had its share of dirty work, and always will, as long as such vast amounts of money are involved. A century and a half on, the 1980s have seen wholesale race fixing in Hong Kong, doping in England and criminal cases against jockeys in the United States, but nothing to rival the events of the 1840s.

III
Racing's New World

Queen Victoria was not amused by racing. She wrote in the royal third person to one of the royal tutors in 1872:

It is deeply regretted by all that Ascot should be visited this year by the Prince of Wales, and The Queen has done all she can to prevent it, but in vain. It is not because the Queen thinks races the dullest things in the world that she is so anxious that the Prince of Wales should discountenance them as much as possible, but on account of the horrible gambling, the ruin to hundreds of families and the heart-breaking of parents caused thereby, which lowers the higher classes frightfully.

But for once the Prince of Wales was prepared to risk maternal wrath and defy Her Majesty's wishes. He shrewdly conjured up another of his mother's anathemas, blithely telling her that it was better to elevate a national sport by bestowing his royal patronage than to 'win the approval of Lord Shaftesbury and the Low Church party' by abstaining from it. And indeed racing's transformation from the roistering and frequently villainous occupation of the first two thirds of the nineteenth century into the fashionable and lordly sport of today can be ascribed in significant measure to its adoption by 'Bertie' in those affluent days of his early manhood.

The great racecourses of Ascot, Epsom, Goodwood, Doncaster and Newmarket saw him thirty or forty times a year. His mistresses were courted there. He brought not only enthusiasm, but standards. When Lady Florence Dixie appeared at Ascot in a tentlike white 'boating dress', he asked her loudly whether she had come in error in her nightgown. He advised a gentleman in mourning that he could not go to Ascot 'where one must wear a top hat. But Newmarket is all right because you can wear a soft hat there.'

Much of the scandal and intrigue of late Victorian England was conducted at the races. It was during a St Leger house party in Yorkshire that the Prince became involved in the

Overleaf
Start of the 1844 Derby
JOHN FREDERICK HERRING
with Leander (green with white sleeves) Running Rein (all white) Ugly Buck (black, orange cap) and Ratan (white with red cap).

Tranby Croft affair in which he had to give evidence in open court about illegal baccarat play. It was at Epsom after Persimmon's Derby victory that the Prince finally buried the decade-old enmity with the Beresford family which had blown up over his affair with Daisy Warwick. Lily Langtry, the first and most splendid of the Prince's mistresses, became a devotee of racing, intervening with the Prince to prevent him moving his trainer Richard Marsh out of Egerton House at Newmarket, and ending up owning two Cesarewitch winners herself, with twenty or more horses in training. This gilded circle of royal favour attracted the most powerful and ambitious men and women of England's most confident age. Lily herself attracted, after the Prince's ardour cooled, the attentions of George Baird, a Scottish multi-millionaire who raced under the name of Mr Abington. His colt Merry Hampton won the 1887 Derby. Violent as well as eccentric, Baird once blacked Lily Langtry's eye. In penitence he bought her a steam yacht, *White Ladye*, twice as big as the Prince of Wales's yacht. He also gave her a very good horse, Milford.

Lily Langtry raced under the diaphanous pseudonym of 'Mr Jersey'. Emil Adam painted one of her best horses, Merman, wearing her silks near the start of the Bunbury mile. Merman won the Cesarewitch at Newmarket as well as the 1899 Jockey Club Cup, the Goodwood Cup, and the Grand Prix at Deauville, where Lily sojourned with her yacht in August.

Emil Adam (1843–1924) came from Munich, and was already an established artist when he came to England to paint for the racing dukes, as well as for Lord Derby and the Prince of Wales. The study of Merman, a glorious liver chestnut, is an immaculate and, no doubt, extremely accurate picture, for Adam was considered pre-eminent as a portrait artist of horses in his day. But like many of his pictures it seems devoid of emotion or enjoyment. The array of his pictures on the walls of the Jockey Club's grand dining room at Newmarket have a distant and passionless air. They give a lofty chill to that most imposing of rooms, in contrast to the vivacious work of Sartorius, Stubbs and Marshall which adds such splendour to that enviable institution.

The courts of Europe in this era were interlinked by family ties, and society in Paris, Vienna or on the Riviera had become, with the arrival of the railways, comfortably international. The *haut monde* of all Europe was drawn into racing on the tails of the

Lily Langtry's Merman
EMIL ADAM

Prince of Wales. The Derby roll, which for the first half of the century had been the preserve of gamblers, rustic gentry and high livers, now became a mirror of the *Almanach de Gotha*. The Dukes of Westminster and Portland were joined by the Baron de Rothschild, Lord Rosebery, Baron de Hirsch. Pierre Lorillard, venturing to England from his successes in the United States, the Chevalier Ginistrelli from Italy, and the Joels, returning hugely rich from the gold and diamond fields of South Africa, all ventured in to racing.

In France, racing grew out of the contests between young bloods on the Champ de Mars in Paris in the 1820s and 30s — indeed Géricault received his fatal injury during a joust there in 1823. These gentlemen jockeys formed the Société d'Encouragement de l'Amélioration des Races de Chevaux en France in 1833. Their principal project was to establish the racecourse at Longchamp in the Bois de Boulogne, so close to the centre of Paris that even the most languid social butterfly would not be '*trop ennuyé*' by distance or country airs. Ever since, the French racing world has cultivated style among its devotees as relentlessly as it has pursued speed among its horses.

The project in the Bois enjoyed the support of Napoleon III and the Comte de Morny. Among the prominent owners engaged in matching or surpassing all that was best in English racing were Auguste Lupin, whose red silks and black cap were to grace the Paris Turf for sixty years, the Comte de Vaublanc, the Comte d'Hedouville, and Alexandre Aumont. The opening of Longchamp coincided in felicitous precision with the arrival of the first great French thoroughbreds. Alexandre Aumont sold all his racehorses to Comte Frédéric de Lagrange, who was thought to be acting for the Emperor himself. Among the colts was Monarque, who was not only to triumph at Longchamp but go to England and bring home the Goodwood Cup. Monarque sired Gladiateur who won the Grand Prix de Paris for Comte de Lagrange, the English Derby, the 2,000 Guineas *and* the St Leger.

In a few seasons Longchamp became the magnet for all Paris. A hundred and fifty thousand people saw Gladiateur's Grand Prix. The prize was more than 100,000 francs. The stands and lawns beside the windmill contrived the most exhilarating panorama. From the day it opened in April 1857, Longchamp attracted artists who then followed the French racing circuit round the year.

Alfred de Dreux (1810–60), entranced in much of his painting with snorting, prancing

Opposite
Return from the Race
ALFRED DE DREUX

66

horses, was caught up too in the triumphs and travails of the racecourse. His horseman and dog returning from the race, bent into the wind and rain, is a soulful reminder that not all is glory in racing.

English artists, too, found a lucrative trade across the Channel. Harry Hall (1814–82), who followed J. F. Herring as the premier painter of racehorses in England, had a house and a well-established clientèle at Newmarket. But he was frequently tempted to Paris. A number of his works still hang there in the rue du Cirque at the headquarters of the Société d'Encouragement, and as early as 1863 he was commissioned by the Marquis de Montgomery to paint his filly La Toucques at Chantilly, where she had won the French Derby. She also won the Prix Diane and the Prix Royal Oak as well as travelling to win the Grosser Preis von Baden, thus permitting her owner to take the waters, and recoup the costs of his sojourn.

So popular had racing become with the masses in both England and France that by 1856 the astute agent and picture engraver Ernest Gambart had recognised that a print of the scene on Derby Day would be a commercial certainty. He and the art collector Jacob Bell laid out £3,000 to commission William Powell Frith (1819–1909) to produce a painting 'five or six feet long' based on sketches Frith had made at Epsom the year before. Frith had once seen the awful consequences of gambling to which his Sovereign was later to allude. He had seen a man at Hampton Court racecourse try to cut his throat with a carving knife. 'Though the man injured himself considerably, judging from the ghastly pallor of his face, and the awful evidence on his beringed hands, I did not believe his attempt was fatal. I heard afterwards that he had been a heavy loser.'

Frith was not greatly interested in horse racing itself, indeed the horses in the background of his Derby Day pictures were copied from sketches sent to him at his request by his friend John Herring. But he was greatly intrigued by the hucksters, the acrobats, the minstrels and, with his notorious eye for the ladies, the 'carriages filled with pretty women'. Frith and his friend Egg were almost taken in by the thimble riggers practising a version of 'find-the-lady' using cups instead of cards. 'So convinced was I that I could find the pea under the thimble that I was on the point of backing my guess rather heavily, when I was stopped by Egg, whose interference was resented by a clerical-looking personage, in language much opposed to what would have been anticipated from one of his cloth.'

Previous page
Derby Day
WILLIAM POWELL FRITH

Marquis de Montgomery's Filly La Toucques at Chantilly HARRY HALL

Frith worked on the painting using a parade of lady models sent to him by Jacob Bell, an acrobat from a Drury Lane pantomime, and a little jockey called Bundy who sat on a wooden horse in the studio.

The result, which was exhibited at the Royal Academy in 1858, is a panorama of wonderful vivacity: the gypsy girl and the louche gentlemen; the thimble riggers and the array of 'pretty women in carriages'. The acrobat is centre stage, appealing to a disinterested picnicker. Each figure in the uproarious crowd is the liveliest of portraits.

Ernest Gambart had already begun teasing the public, whom he hoped would buy the prints, with sneak previews and articles in the popular magazines. The picture was destined to be a *succès fou* even before opening day. Frith's diary records: 'Never was such a crowd seen round a picture. The secretary obliged to get a policeman to keep people off. He is to be there from eight in the morning.' Gambart, delighted, was nevertheless alarmed to see his investment in imminent danger of damage as the policeman's coat buttons were pressed towards the canvas. Ever the publicist, he pressed for the one thing he knew would cause divisive horror at the Academy — an iron rail round the picture. It had only been done once before, when many Academicians suffered the vapours at such distinction being awarded to Sir David Wilkie's painting of Waterloo in 1822. But the rail arrived. So did the Queen and the Prince Consort — the latter offering constructive comments as to the balance of light and shade, which Frith loyally says he adopted to improve the picture after the exhibition.

Derby Day then set off on a year-long progress round not only Britain but much of the world, drawing crowds wherever it went, before being sent to Paris to be engraved by Auguste Blanchard, and the copies to be marketed almost as enthusiastically as they had been in England. For racing in France, formally initiated only twenty years earlier by the gentlemen who formed the Société d'Encouragement, had already attained a grandeur and *chic* that left the rougher standards of contemporary England far behind.

The eighteenth-century background of the Château de Chantilly and the new Longchamp track in the fashionable environs of the Bois de Boulogne imbued French race meetings from the start with an elegance which attracted the French aristocracy as much as the owners. The Marquis de Breteuil, the Marquis de Jaucourt, the Comtesse de Pourtales all played host to the Prince of Wales at the Paris race meetings, which attracted him almost as much as the night clubs and the variety theatres. Pierre Gavarni's

Opposite
Races at Longchamp 1874
PIERRE GAVARNI

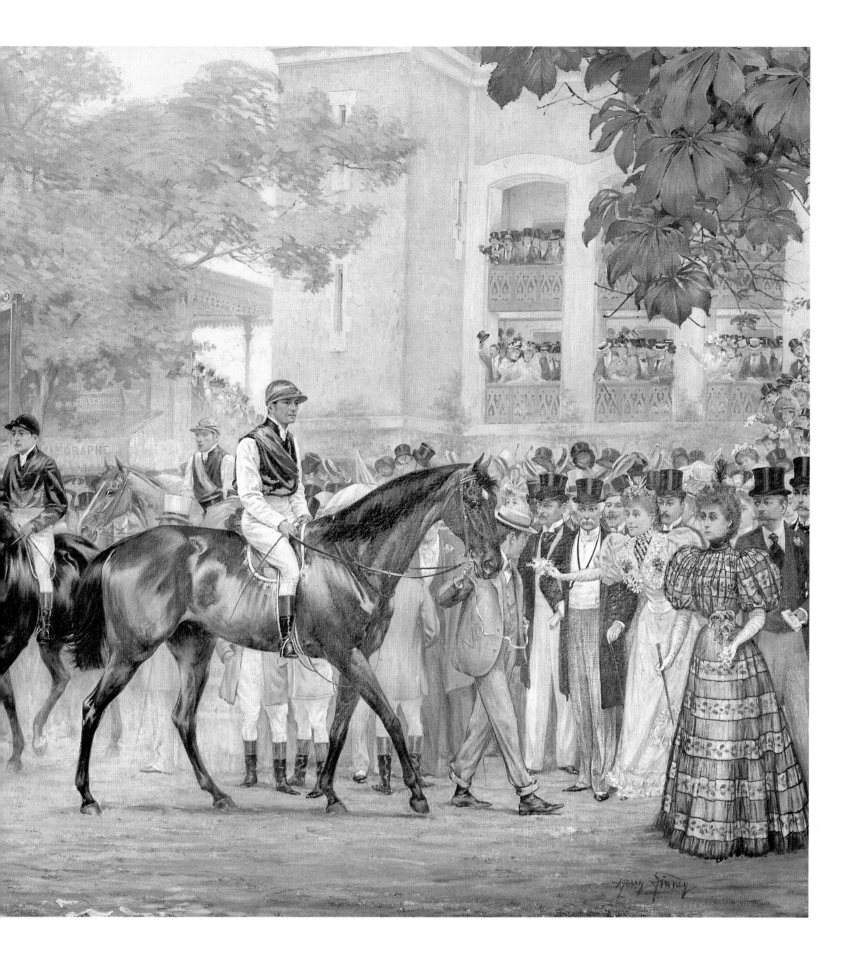

picture of a meeting at Longchamp in 1874 is a parade of grace and fashion: hats, gowns and parasols of ostentatious splendour; a hand languorously awaiting the replenishment of the champagne; the conversation, the gossip and the badinage evidently immensely more fascinating than the passing show on the Turf itself. Scarcely a soul seems to be interested in the thoroughbred going by on the rails.

Peter le Bihan's (*fl.* 1860–70) picture of Longchamp racecourse in 1862 portrays great joie de vivre, with animation in almost every one of the tiny figures: the lady on the white Arab in imminent danger of capsizing, her consort already parted from his top hat; two expansive gestures implying '*Zut alors!*' from the lady with the parasol and her companion in the foreground; a tempted but reluctant customer for the pieman, and a pompous pipe-smoking interlocutor for the cavalryman. The purposeful line of enthusiasts marches in from the left, intent on reaching the action in front of the imposing new grandstand, while fashionable ladies swirl across the turf. It is a picture unstriking at first glance, yet redolent in its every detail of the eager atmosphere of an enjoyable day at the most popular new outdoor entertainment in Paris.

Harry Finney's vast and joyful picture of Longchamp at the turn of the century is also suffused with the pleasure of it all. There is a sea of silk toppers, with one dandy in grey. There is the wonderfully pretty lady in blue, wasp waisted and animated. Legend has it that it is Mistinguett. A lady in a blue hat is handing a nosegay to a surprised lad leading a horse. Twenty years from one war and twenty years before the next, the soldiers stand out in careless confidence. The horses belong to some of the great names of French racing.

This picture hangs, appositely, in the club house of America's most elegant racecourse at Keeneland, Kentucky. England has its Ascot, and America its spring in Keeneland and its summer sojourn at Saratoga. But nowhere is racing so inextricably entwined with fashion, society and the social round as in France. Today, as for more than a century now, the racing world progresses in the spring from Longchamp to the Château de Chantilly, then to the long August weeks beside the sea at Deauville, and back to Paris for the autumn.

These days, with the Prix de l'Arc de Triomphe established as the greatest race in Europe, there is a last glorious fling at the end of September or in the first days of

Previous page
The Paddock at Longchamp
HARRY FINNEY

Longchamp 1862 PETER LE BIHAN

October. All Paris has returned from the holidays — and half of England flown over too, it sometimes seems — and there is the most glittering display of fashion and extravagance beneath the trees of Longchamp's paddock. This is not the Ascot pantomime of absurd hats and morning coats, nor the laid-back champagne breakfasts of Saratoga, but a parade of the magnificence of the Paris jewellers, of St Laurent and Cardin, arrayed before the finest bloodstock in Europe.

French and European painters who have otherwise shown no special devotion to horseflesh have frequently been drawn to the racetrack. Jacques Villon's (1875–1963) picture of horses at Chantilly in 1950 is a hypnotic Mondrian-like composition of colour, shape and movement. Kees van Dongen (1877–1968) constantly returned to the race track for studies like his precipitous picture *Blue Grass Races*, with scudding clouds and

Opposite
The Races
PIERRE BONNARD

Deauville Races
JEAN LOUIS FORAIN

Horseback Riding, Chantilly
JACQUES VILLON

Opposite
Blue Grass Races
KEES VAN DONGEN

the horses cascading down the canvas. Jean Louis Forain (1832–1931) produced a lovely watercolour at Deauville races. The horse is well enough done but the scene is dominated by the haughty lady in black and her companion with his yellow buttonhole. Even Pierre Bonnard (1867–1947), going to the races in 1894 and painting the horses milling about before the off, could not resist permitting the starter himself to dominate the canvas. Firmly at attention, the ample and immaculate figure waits for the jockeys to sort themselves out. Even from this rear view there is a glimpse of his moustache. The bright red flag is ready behind his back.

But the most assiduous and entranced portrayer of racing's social scene was Raoul Dufy (1877–1953). At Deauville, Longchamp and Chantilly, and then across the Channel at Epsom and Ascot he followed the caravanserai. Alongside his picture of Ascot in 1935 in the Mellon collection, there is a fascinating series of thirty-eight pencil drawings that he made at the racecourse as studies for the painting, together with notes on colour and clothing. The sketches are very strong, and simple lines evoke character in two or three strokes. Many of them have been transferred precisely to the painting.

To Dufy the races were an open air salon. The theatre was among the crowd, not in the contest on the track. The colour and the opulence were invested in the spectators, and

80

not in the expensive bloodstock on the track. It is left to others to worship the horse. Only a handful of the thirty-eight sketches are of the horses or the racecourse itself.

The extended round of the English racing season from Doncaster in the north to Goodwood on the south coast demanded an almost professional dedication from owners and enthusiasts. Sir John Astley described the arrangements necessary to 'do Newmarket proper', as he described it, in the 1870s. He bought a cottage and little paddock from Robinson the jockey. He and his wife each had two hacks. Every fine morning they would be out on the Limekilns to watch work, and back home for breakfast around ten thirty.

> An hour or so before the races we mounted our fresh hacks, and with a fly to carry our coats, cloaks and convey our two grooms, we caracoled down to the races, seldom dismounting, but riding from saddling paddock to betting ring, and backwards and forwards between different courses. If it rained real hard, we hopped off into our fly.

Sadly this lifestyle required better luck in the betting ring than was usually Sir John's lot. 'It was a bitter blow when, in after years, the nicest little crib at Newmarket had to be sold. Jockey Wood bought it.'

In the following decade Newmarket received the accolade which finally established it as the leading training ground in England and the Headquarters, as it likes to describe itself, of racing: the Prince of Wales moved all his horses from John Porter's gallops at Kingsclere in Hampshire to the sumptuous Egerton House in Newmarket, which had been built by Richard Marsh. There, a precise ritual would be conducted when the Prince came with his entourage and Lord Marcus Beresford, his racing manager, to look round the horses in the afternoons. First it was whisky on the lawn, weather permitting, then an inquisition of Marsh before embarking on a tour of the stables themselves. The move to Newmarket changed the Prince's racing luck, which had been lamentable. He had only won one race by 1886 — and one of his horses, the filly Counterpane, really had dropped dead in the finishing straight while well in the lead. It was a cup race at Stockbridge.

In the spring and autumn there were important sales up North in the less glamorous surroundings of Doncaster. Lowes Dickinson (1819–1908) and Myles Birket Foster (1825–99) nevertheless thought it worth venturing a subscription picture of this

Ascot RAOUL DUFY

unpromising occasion, so deeply was the whole business of the thoroughbred by then embedded in society. The rickety roof, the peeling railings, the open air ring all take this picture of Doncaster sales in about 1885 far from the atmosphere of Ascot or Longchamp. The Tattersalls are auctioning yearlings, and much of the *beau monde* as well as the racing world is present; the Dukes of Westminster and Portland, the Countess of Zetland and Viscountess Newport have all presumably contributed to having their portraits painted as well as the great names of the weighing room, trainers and jockeys. There are Dawsons, Darlings, Arnulls, I'Anson, Cannon, Elsey and, moustachioed in the left foreground, the redoubtable Captain Machell who bought Hermit and made a fortune out of that most unlikely of Derby winners — for Hermit had broken a major blood vessel only a week before the race. Behind the ring is the rakish white hat of Monsieur Le Fièvre, disturbing the phalanx of toppers and bowlers, and squarely with his back to the painter, as likely a gesture of impecuniousness as defiance, is Sir John Astley. Sir John, known to all as 'The Mate', was ruined by a big gamble on his horse Peter in the 1881 Manchester Cup. It cost him twelve thousand pounds. But for fifty years he had been one of the great characters of the Turf. No subscription painter could afford to leave him out.

Sir John Astley's friend, the young Duke of Portland, had affable memories of that era, when Newmarket held sway. 'When I first went to Newmarket I lived in a little house in the High Street. Lord Enniskillen, Lord Lurgan, Lord Rocksavage, Lord Berkeley Paget and Lord Charles Beresford were often my guests there, and we used to invite many friends to dinner. Our ideas of hospitality nearly always exceeded the capacity of our room and dinner table; and on several occasions some of us had to dine at the piano.' Fifty years on he still relished in retrospect the morning hacks to see the racehorses, and the breakfast when they came back. 'Even now I can taste the prawns and Newmarket sausages we used to devour. In those now far-off days racing society was extremely pleasant. I have no doubt that it still is so, but *autres temps, autres gens, autres moeurs.*'

Those were not merely an old man's rose-tinted memories of halcyon days. For, a century later, it is certain that the Duke was living through not only one of the great eras of racing society, but also one of the great epochs of the thoroughbred. The Duke himself, through the sad but serendipitous accident of Prince Batthyany dying literally in his arms on Newmarket racecourse, acquired perhaps the greatest horse since Eclipse, St

Tattersalls' Sale at Doncaster
MYLES BIRKET FOSTER and LOWES DICKINSON

Simon. St Simon was never beaten, indeed his jockey took a mile to pull him up at Goodwood, and he sired ten winners of seventeen English classics, thus stamping his line for ever on the stud book. One of St Simon's sons out of the mare Perdita II was Persimmon, owned by the Prince of Wales.

The Duke also owned Donovan, Ayrshire, and the great stallion Carbine whom he bought by telegram, sight unseen, from Australia for £13,000. Carbine was not only to get the Derby winner Spearmint, but also to inject the old Camel-Touchstone blood into the dam's line which produced through Nearco the dominant thoroughbred blood of the modern era. The Duke festooned his house, Welbeck Abbey, with portraits of his horses by the likes of Robert Alexander and Lynwood Palmer, George Wright Barker and Charles Lutyens, Alfred Grenfell Haigh and Thomas P. Earl as well as many by Emil Adam.

The half century before the First World War was in many ways the heyday of English racing: great horses; huge crowds; royal patronage; enviable affluence. Yet, unlike in France, the leading artists of the day showed but vestigial interest in racing. The full-blooded amusements of the racecourse, the flamboyant show of racing society, the magnificence of the thoroughbred horse, so beguiling to Rowlandson and Herring before, and to Munnings and Skeaping afterwards, were unlikely to touch a chord with the ethereal concerns of Pre-Raphaelites or Neo-Classicists, or any of the Victorian schools which now seem so remote from the mainstream of modern art. Even the narrative painters rarely ventured into territory which certainly offered commercial attractions.

The most noted animal painter of the day, Sir Edwin Landseer, only painted one racehorse, the Marquis of Zetland's Voltigeur, and the commission took the ageing peer years of begging and pleading to achieve. In the end the heroic St Leger winner and victor of the great match against the Flying Dutchman at York had to be trundled 250 miles south to Landseer's London studio before his likeness could be recorded on canvas. After Frith's great success with *Derby Day* — and he found it worthwhile painting a number of almost full-size copies — it was as though the well was considered drunk dry by his Academician colleagues.

Opposite
The Paddock
RAOUL DUFY

Ascot 1935   Raoul Dufy

IV
America

In the boom years from 1860 onwards racing enjoyed an extraordinary growth of popularity in the United States. Saratoga Springs in upstate New York became the summer resort for the wealthy of Manhattan and the East Coast, with racing throughout most of the three-month summer season.

Today, August at Saratoga, leading up to the climax of the Travers Stakes, is as appealing, relaxed and elegant a month of racing as any in the world, with its indulgent routine of champagne breakfasts while watching the morning work at the track, saddling

The United States Hotel, Saratoga

under the trees for the afternoon's contests, and opera, concerts and galas in the evening. Yet it seems a pale shadow compared with the Saratoga of a century ago. The waters of the spa springs, the casinos and the racetrack made the headiest of cocktails and lured the richest families in America.

The United States Hotel, opened in 1874, was the most palatial symbol of Saratoga's appeal, and became the headquarters of the racing set. With a dining room that could seat a thousand, 768 bedrooms, and cottages for 'discreet' entertaining, it offered the most luxurious lifestyle in America. It is extraordinary to recall that while this hotel was lavishing its libations on the racegoers of New York, Geronimo was still loose on the other side of the country, and General Custer had yet to ride to his last stand.

There is a romantic, histrionic quality to American equestrian painting in the latter half of the nineteenth century, almost as though a soundtrack should be accompanying the pictures. For it was a form of painting attuned to the explosive growth of money, leisure and prosperity in the East, yet born out of the art of adventure and endeavour in the West which had so excited urban America from the days when George Catlin opened his Indian Gallery in New York and Washington in 1837. Catlin was followed by Arthur Fitzwilliam Tait, whose predelictions ran to hunting sagas and lone battles with grizzlies, but who never actually went west of Chicago, and Seth Eastman, a soldier based in Texas, who really did know the Indians he sketched.

But it was Frederic Remington (1861–1909) above all who brought the dramas of the Indians and the Plains, and the mounted heroes of the West to the picture- and print-buying city dwellers of the East. Remington, a native New Yorker, went West after his sheep ranch in Kansas failed. He made an epic ride from the Gala River in New Mexico through the whole span of the United States to the Indian territories in the Dakotas. Returning to New York, his paintings, full of bravado and the authentic feel of the West, enjoyed a tremendous success.

Scarcely surprising then that when Remington turned to racing, his work should have all the hot-blooded vigour which infused his Western paintings. His picture *The Start* was inspired, he recorded, by an incident at the new Sheepshead Bay track at Coney Island, New York. It is, in fact, a false start. The two outside horses are being pulled up as though they were rodeo animals. The negro jockey in the middle has more control, and his expression suggests that he does not expect to see his rivals survive in the saddle. It is a picture constructed for instant impact, the horses dashing towards the viewer — and indeed this painting, like so many others of that era, was designed for the popular magazines of the time, *Harper's Weekly, Collier's,* and *Leslie's Weekly.*

Remington's racing pictures are few — there is another of steeplechasing at Cedarhurst — but they are born of first-hand experience and pulsate with life. Cedarhurst, on Long Island, was known as 'the largest country club in America', and was one of the birthplaces of steeplechasing in the United States. The Rockaway Hunt Club, founded in 1877, had

Steeplechase at Cedarhurst FREDERIC REMINGTON

The Start FREDERIC REMINGTON

by 1884 established a permanent chasing course and clubhouse, and there is no mistaking the gentlemanly style of the moustachioed riders in Remington's picture, as they boast a supernatural poise over the water jump below.

Louis Maurer (1832–1932) was another artist who sought to portray the headier excitements of the racetrack. Maurer was an extraordinary man. He arrived in New York in 1850, at the age of eighteen, from Biebrich in the Rhineland and started work as a lithographer. He lived to be a hundred. He was a concert-standard flautist, owned his own printing works, was an authority on sea shells and a crack shot who won a marksmanship contest at the age of ninety. He did not turn to painting until he was forty, but thereafter was a dedicated and industrious artist, enrolling at Gotham Art School when he was fifty to improve his technique and mounting a one-man exhibition when he was ninety-nine. This ebullient energy and lust for life pervades all his work, both on canvas and in stone. Whether portraying thoroughbred racing or sulkies, Maurer concentrated on the high moments in the final stretch, when the blood of horse and spectator alike was at its quickest.

His painting of the First Futurity at Sheepshead Bay in 1888 captures the moment when the great Salvator was beaten by Proctor Knott in the most valuable race ever yet run. The two negro jockeys, Barnes on Proctor Knott, and Hamilton, are all out at the post with the rest of the field, bar Galen, almost distanced. Proctor Knott won $40,000 that day, more than any other horse was to win all year.

The Coney Island Jockey Club's cunning scheme to raise the money invited owners of mares to nominate a foal, as soon as it was conceived, to run for the Futurity three years later when it was two years old. The initial fee was modest and 752 owners indulged in this unlikely but inviting gamble in 1885, more than half a year before the foals were even born. Of the 752, just fourteen went to the post in 1888. The Coney Island Jockey Club added $10,000, and the scene was set for the hectic contest which Maurer painted.

It is a huge and populist picture, glorying in the atmosphere of a day on which publicity and showmanship culminated in triumph, a day worthy of the fairground fame which Coney Island was to acquire. The elegant two-tier judges' stand, the symbol of Sheepshead Bay, is a splendid eyrie for the officials. In the background the packed crowds have their hats off waving in appreciation — how polite were expressions of excitement in those times!

Previous page
The First Futurity
LOUIS MAURER

94

The pattern of the Sheepshead Bay Futurity proved an enduring innovation and even in the 1980s it provided the basic template for the American Breeders' Cup series, where each race is worth a million dollars or more.

Proctor Knott was the one horse Salvator could never manage to beat. Otherwise Salvator was practically invincible throughout his career as a three- and four-year-old, usually ridden by the black jockey Isaac Murphy. Black jockeys have almost disappeared from American race tracks, but a century ago they were as prominent as the Latin American riders of today.

Isaac Murphy, who won three Kentucky Derbys, was immortalised in silver by Ed Hamilton, the Kentucky sculptor, and, along with Salvator, in a breathless poem by Ella Wheeler Wilcox, after the great match against Tenny at Sheepshead Bay in 1890.

Isaac Murphy
ED HAMILTON

> One more mighty plunge, and with knee, limb and hand
> I lift my horse first by a nose past the stand.
> We are under the string now — the great race is done
> And Salvator, Salvator, Salvator won.

This race, for $5,000 a side, reflected the almost frenetic enthusiasm for racing in that era, so graphically reflected in Maurer's paintings. As the *Spirit of the Times* put it: 'It is useless to tell people that the only reason people go to see races is to make money. No amounts of money could have induced the cheering, yelling, waving of handkerchiefs, clapping of hands and irresistible outbursts which infected even the most decorous — and ladies as much as any.'

Maurer's son Alfred was prominent in the Cubist movement, anathema to his father. Alfred had to live with both his father's disapproval and the bitter pill of Louis's continuing nonagenarian success. Shortly after Louis's death and the encomiums which followed, Alfred committed suicide, despairing, perhaps, of ever matching his father's fame and fortune.

Foremost of the people's painters was Henry Stull (1851–1913), who for more than forty years conveyed to the owners, patrons and readers of *Leslie's Weekly* the thrills of the New York tracks. Stull was a considerable figure in Eastern racing society. He had a

95

Beldame HENRY STULL

studio on Broadway near Madison Square. His colours of white, gold sash and cuffs and black cap were familiar on the New York tracks, notably with a colt named Valentino, by Virgil. And he travelled regularly to England and France, accompanying Pierre Lorillard the year he brought Iroquois to Epsom to win the Derby.

Stull's picture of the 1900 Brighton Cup shows Perry Belmont's colt Ethelbert beating the Imp. This was a revenge match, for Imp had beaten Ethelbert the previous year, and after two and a quarter miles Ethelbert only prevailed by a head. Stull understood his audience. This picture is how racing lives in the exalted halls of memory — clouds of dust, and two huge thoroughbreds at frightening full stretch, neck and neck. The two jockeys, Spencer on Ethelbert, and Jenkins are curved over the horses' necks in that overweening pose which Stull invariably used when portraying a thoroughbred ridden full out.

Opposite
The Brighton Cup 1900
HENRY STULL

96

He had a shrewd commercial eye for public favourites and a style designed to flatter, even to caricature their qualities and prowess. Imp, the coal black mare in the picture, was the heroine of the day, constantly challenging the colts, often winning, but always running. As a three-year-old she had run in fifty races and been placed in all but seventeen. In all she won sixty-two of her 171 races and was placed in another sixty-four. When she went home to her owner D. R. Harness's house in Chillicothe, Ohio, the town declared a public holiday, and the mare and her jockey Pete Clay paraded through the streets, decked in her racing colours of orange and black.

Stull's picture of Beldame winning the 1904 Saratoga Cup is a classic of Stull hyperbole. Beldame hardly lives up to her name. She is no beauty — awkward and unfurnished — but the picture portrays the very essence of excitement of the galloping horse: eager head; flying plaited tail; the dirt kicked up; sweat on the reins; the jockey curved in his orange and black silks against the lowering, scudding storm clouds. August Belmont, who owned her, had leased her out the year of the Cup victory to Newton Bennington, for whom she won twelve of her fourteen races, being beaten only by older males. Tough mares, however plain, have always appealed to the racing public, whether it be the turn-of-the-century American heroines or, seventy years on, the likes of Dahlia, Allez France, Pebbles and Triptych.

With racing stopped during the Second World War, Saratoga town went into decline. The Grand Union Hotel disappeared in 1952, the United States Hotel had already gone, the casinos were closed. But the racing was mercifully saved through the acquisition of the track by the New York Racing Association in 1955. Their stewardship has been rewarded by the presence of many of the great horses of the post-war era at the summer festival.

For all the boisterous quality of American racing — and the crowds at Aqueduct and Hollywood Park today can be every bit as demonstrative as the Sheepshead Bay contingents of a century ago — there is also a gentler, affectionate, folksy tradition, epitomised by Saratoga, Keeneland in Kentucky, or Santa Anita in California, which has always attracted artists.

Nashua's Farewell to Keeneland
MILTON MENASCO

W. Smithson Broadhead (1888–1960), the Englishman who painted so many scenes at Saratoga, left a mellow memorial of three racing legends in his picture of Nashua in the

98

paddock. As the champion is led past, his trainer Sunny Jim Fitzsimmons is talking to jockey Eddie Arcaro, who won five Kentucky Derbys. Fitzsimmons trained thoroughbreds for nigh on seventy years, and turned out the Triple Crown winners Gallant Fox and Omaha, as well as Bold Ruler and Granville. Gallant Fox came to grief at Saratoga, defeated in mud and rain in the Travers by the 100 to 1 shot Jim Dandy, who lost a dozen other races that year.

Indeed Saratoga has truly been the graveyard of champions. Man o'War met his only defeat there by a horse called Upset in 1919 and in 1973 Secretariat, already Triple Crown champion, came for the Whitney Stakes and lost to a little horse called Onion.

Nashua and his great rival, the chestnut colt Swaps, were the two horses who dominated American racing in 1955 and 1956. Swaps beat Nashua in the Kentucky Derby and then went home to California leaving his victim a free run at the other two classics, the Preakness and the Belmont, on his home ground in the East. This disdainful departure from the field by the triumphant Swaps, followed by Nashua's victories, inevitably fanned the flames of the eternal jousting between East and West coasts which took over from the contests between Yankee and Dixie of a century ago. In 1989 California came again with Sunday Silence to trounce an Eastern champion, Easy Goer, in the first two classics, lose to him in the third, and then triumph in the Breeders' Cup.

For Swaps and Nashua, a showdown was unavoidable. It finally came in the most celebrated match race of the post-war years; a straight $100,000 to the winner. The two colts lined up at Washington Park, Chicago, in 1955 for a race where tactics were of supreme importance. Yelling and thrashing with his whip, Arcaro got Nashua off first and seized the rail. Tantalisingly he opened up half a gap for Swaps on the home turn, then closed it and forced him wide. Nashua was never headed and won the prize with 1 minute 37 ³/₅ for the mile. For the next year he progressed round the most celebrated courses, as the idol of the East, and retired to stud with earnings of $750,000.

In the Saratoga picture of Nashua, Smithson Broadhead has, in Hitchcockian fashion, put a portrait of himself and his wife in the corner of the picture. Broadhead was an Englishman, born and raised in Lancashire and Yorkshire. Though he worked for two decades in England, the overwhelming attraction of his work is in his intoxication with the brilliant light and translucent colours that he encountered in California and the

Opposite
Nashua at Saratoga
W. SMITHSON BROADHEAD

100

Keeneland Paddock
PETER WILLIAMS

deserts of the American West. He first worked across the Atlantic in 1911, then again for five years before the Second World War, then for the years after 1947. His pictures are vivid and distinctive. Nashua's coat shines in a sunlight which has perhaps never in reality graced the heavier climate of upper New York State, but this is the sunshine of Valhalla, preserved from ordinary mortals.

Milton Menasco painted a farewell tribute to Nashua on his last appearance at that most gracious of America's racecourses, Keeneland, Kentucky, where the atmosphere is unsullied by racecourse commentaries, and the sounds of thundering hoofs, gasping horses, and shouting jockeys are bewitchingly enhanced until they are subsumed in the crowd's roar in the final stretch.

The relaxed atmosphere behind the scenes is shown in Elmore J. Brown's (b.1899) picture of the Oklahoma training track across the road from the Saratoga racecourse, a homely sunlit study of the scene which beguiles many summer visitors. The young boy rider, shirt off, shares a cane chair with the old horseman in a Panama hat, as the horse is bridled. The lane of stalls — washing hung out — stretches away down the nave of trees. This is the communion of working horsemen, age and youth in the warmth of a Saratoga afternoon, workaday — upturned buckets, unraked sand — yet full of affection for the horse and the comradeship of horsepeople. Elmore Brown went to school with Ernest Hemingway at Oak Park, Illinois, and illustrated Hemingway's first published short story. This picture of a man's world strikes a Hemingway chord, forty years after that first collaboration.

An earlier artist to represent the restrained, classical, perhaps more European vein in American racing art, was Edward Troye (1808–74), a Swiss who arrived in Philadelphia at the age of twenty-three. Within six months, three paintings he had contributed to the annual exhibition of the Pennsylvania Academy of Fine Arts had launched him on a career painting thoroughbreds for the leading owners in America, and trotters too, which was to last forty years. His exact renderings of conformation, colour, and character appealed to the most demanding owners, and for almost all that time Troye had the field effectively to himself. He was overtaken finally both by photography and by the more raucous tastes of the late nineteenth century. But his work compares favourably with that of any of the contemporaries he left behind in Europe. Troye's spiritual heirs have been Franklin Voss and, in recent times, Richard Stone Reeves (b. 1921).

Opposite
Oklahoma
ELMORE BROWN

The Race Mare Reality
at John Charles Craig's
Stud Farm, 1833
EDWARD TROYE

Tom Fool, American Horse
of the Year, 1954
RICHARD STONE REEVES

V

The Passion for Action

The racing of thoroughbred horses was an inspiration for the Romantic and Impressionist avant-garde of the nineteenth century. The grace, the glamour, the colour, the fevered intensity of the action on the racecourse were irresistible to artists bursting away from the mannered patterns of the Age of Reason.

Géricault (1791–1824), who haunted the shambles of Paris and the prison morgues, sketching in repellent fascination the slaughtered oxen and the guillotined heads of felons, at last found a more sunlit stimulus when he visited Rome in 1817. The race of the riderless horses in Rome, in the early years of the last century, must have been an extraordinary spectacle. Goethe was enthralled by it as the highlight of the Roman carnival, and Géricault saw it as the inspiration for what would have been perhaps the most extraordinary equestrian picture ever painted. He bought a 30-foot-long canvas and began work on a series of studies for a painting which would have overshadowed even his gigantic *Raft of the Medusa* (which is now in the Louvre in Paris).

Sadly, in the swirling currents of Géricault's turbulent life, the canvas was left behind in Rome when he returned to Paris, and the picture was never painted, but his study, now in the Walters Gallery in Baltimore, of the Barbary horses at the start on the Corso is a passionate glimpse of an impassioned event. The horses wear only coloured head plumes. Géricault has captured the supreme tension of the last moments before the off: the arching grey thrusting at the barrier, one leg already over the rope; the plunging chestnut being held back by two men; a couple of horses corralled in starting stalls. The spectators, packed in the tribunes all around, complete the cauldron of excitement. As with the Palio in Siena, the horses were supported by different sections of the city, and the gambling was prodigious.

This is a picture out of time. The blood is racing. There is the high emotion which the

Race of the Riderless Horses in Rome THEODORE GERICAULT

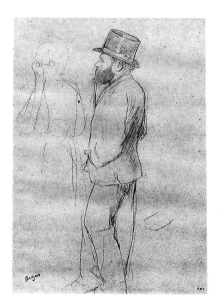

Manet at the Races
EDGAR DEGAS

twentieth-century painters were to capture in the action of the racecourse. But this is 1817. Géricault was to go to England three years later, and to admire not only Constable — he told Delacroix later that he had been 'intoxicated' by one of the Suffolk landscapes — but also the skilled and more sober English horse painters, notably James Pollard. Indeed he painted a picture of the Epsom Derby in 1821 very much in acknowledgement of Pollard's famous print of Sir Joshua beating Filho da Puta. The layout of the picture is conventional. But the whole scene is dedicated to the impression of action: the scudding skies; the jockeys driving into their saddles; the horses themselves, despite the rocking horse action, in convincing and furious competition.

Géricault has been hailed as the precursor of the modern movement, as the forerunner of Impressionism in France, the inspiration for Delacroix and his followers. Certainly he was the first great painter of horses in action. And it was horses which killed him. First a fall when his horse refused at a gate, and then a collision during a race on the Champ de Mars, which aggravated the injury. He died in 1824, aged thirty-two, having exhibited only three pictures in his lifetime but leaving behind another four hundred, including two of racing's first true action pictures, described above.

But it was the Impressionists — Manet, Degas, and Toulouse-Lautrec — who found a lasting fascination in racing. The very year, 1856, that Manet (1832–83) was jousting with his teacher about the immense power of light and colour — 'Even the shadows are coloured,' he proclaimed — the great racecourse at Longchamp in Paris was being laid out. Racing was to lure some of the most superb 'coloured shadows' from Manet, and perhaps the first great emotional pictures of action on the racecourse. There is a splendid sketch by Degas of Manet at the races. He is a dandy, with topper and cane, not at all the dishevelled flamboyant, intent on the day's proceedings.

For horsemen, the first sight of one of Manet's great racing paintings is sensational. *At The Races*, painted in 1875, was a product of that tempest of exhilaration when Manet accompanied the young Monet and Renoir to the village of Argenteuil near Paris to paint in the bright open air, beside the River Seine. In that long summer of 1874, Manet found a new inspiration. The enchantment of painting out of doors in the ever-changing light gave his work a new vigour. *At The Races*, with its hypnotic blue tone and dense green background, is powerful enough. But the effect of the action is overwhelming. The

110

Racing at Epsom THEODORE GERICAULT

horses have just passed the winning post, and they come careering straight out of the picture, head on, in a frantic scramble to pull up before the boundary fence. The light bay in the leading couple is already plunging and splaying across the track, the jockey behind hauling on the reins to avoid the maelstrom in front.

The picture has a dizzying impact. It seems totally modern. By choosing to paint the horses from the front, Manet has evaded the curse of the 'rocking horse' gallop. The horses are the boldest of impressions cascading out of the funnel of fence and crowd. It was perhaps the first great painting truly to succeed in distilling the excitement and the action of racing on to canvas.

As many a foot-soldier must have known, the sight of horses hurtling head on is a heart-stopping experience, and perhaps the most difficult of all to depict. Lady Butler was to bring it off a few years later with *Scotland For Ever*, her picture of the charge of the Scots Greys at Waterloo, and in 1898 Alexander Wagner produced his monumental *Chariot Race*, with its extraordinary 3-D effect which makes it best viewed from a distance of fifty paces or more. Wagner's picture has been the inspiration for all those epics of canvas and screen from Ben Hur onward which exploit the terror of thundering hoofs and the savagery of the arena. But Manet's picture is a superb synthesis of that new approach which the Impressionists brought to art and the new excitements which thoroughbred racing was bringing to the cosmopolitan crowds of nineteenth-century Paris.

Edgar Degas (1834–1917), Manet's companion at the racetrack, was concerned with the more contained moments before the off, the laconic circling of horses behind the start line as they wait for stragglers to appear, or the final tensions as the horses, hard on the bit, crowd in to the start line. Degas made early studies around 1860, pencil drawings of horses which decades later he was to incorporate into racing paintings.

Before the Start, set in blustery weather against a distant industrial landscape, is full of edgy anticipation as the horses walk in to the line. It would seem to be a gentleman's race, the jockeys with patrician beards, upright in the saddle with that unbending seat which distinguishes the amateur, however capable, from the louche and looser posture of the professional. Degas' pictures, always crowded with horses like a Roman frieze, carefully patterned and full of colour, are full of the ritual of racing.

At the Races EDOUARD MANET

Horse and Jockey — The End of the Race EDGAR DEGAS

Degas described himself as 'the classical painter of modern life' and devoted prolonged and intense study not only to copying the old masters but to carefully drawing and sketching every detail of the contemporary scenes with which he was concerned. His pencil drawings of horses, made while he was in his early twenties, are meticulous studies which were to be the foundation of his mature paintings and, in his final years, of the bronzes. He was thus well prepared when it fell to him to be the first significant artist to make use of the revelatory photographic work of Eadweard Muybridge in America.

It is extraordinary but incontrovertible that no artist in all the millennia since horses were first drawn on the walls of caves had understood how a horse walks, trots, canters, and gallops. When the early books on equestrianism like the Duke of Newcastle's *Master of the Horse* were published, they concentrated notably on control of the different gaits of the horse. Young riders must always have been taught to know with which leg their horse was leading, or how to change legs at the trot or canter. These are fundamentals of equestrianism, which become instinctive to the experienced rider. Yet there seems to be no evidence that generation after generation of artistic patrons, let alone artists, realised the falseness of the 'rocking horse' gallop, by which horses were portrayed with front legs splayed forward and hind legs backwards — a position which they never remotely approach in real life.

Muybridge took his famous photographs, using twenty-four cameras in line with a trip thread to activate them as the horse went by, in order to settle a wager struck by Governor Leland Stanford, builder of the Central Pacific Railroad. The results astonished

Previous page
The Chariot Race
ALEXANDER WAGNER

116

Horse with Lowered Head EDGAR DEGAS

the equestrian world, won Stanford his bet by showing that trotting horses really do have all four feet off the ground at some point, and launched Muybridge on a career in which he took photographs of dogs and many other animals in action, and then of humans, sitting, walking, and running — photographs that were almost as influential to the artistic world as the equine sequences.

Muybridge took to the road with his zoopraxiscope, a rotating projector which he devised for displaying his work, and gave demonstrations all along the East Coast and then in London and Paris. The pictures were published in an article in 1878 and then in full in Muybridge's great volume *Animal Locomotion*, in 1887. As soon as he saw them,

Sequence from
Animal Locomotion
EADWEARD MUYBRIDGE

117

Degas took an intense interest in Muybridge's photographs, copying them fastidiously in chalk and pencil, and then using the drawings for his late racing pictures, which have a vigour and confidence in movement which is quite different from his early work.

Degas was fascinated too by the characteristic quirks of racehorses, the way they stretch their necks and pull at their jockeys before a race, and then demand relaxation and reward in similar fashion once the contest is over. After Muybridge and Degas, no artist could credibly persist with the ancient conventions of the horse in action. Toulouse-Lautrec (1864–1901), so devoted to capturing moments of high excitement in the theatre, the cabaret or the circus, found another arena beyond Montmartre, in the racing at Longchamp, and produced some wonderfully exact and effusive sketches of horses and jockeys. Even in exile Gauguin (1848–1903) could not resist a Tahitian tribute to Degas in his 1902 painting *Riders on the Beach*.

Patrons, however, were perhaps not educated as swiftly as artists, and indeed may have found certain representations of the galloping horse grotesque, especially those which showed it with all its legs tucked up, like some airborne hedgehog. Indeed, to this day, it is rare to see this pose presented on canvas.

It might be fair to surmise that the Irish Colonel Harry McCalmont was one of that conservative persuasion. In 1893, his Isonomy colt Isinglass won the Derby at Epsom, and the colonel commissioned from Godfrey Giles a huge picture — nearly nine feet wide — which is one of racing's more spectacular panoramas. Isinglass was the result of one of those fortunate chances which recur in racing. His dam Deadlock was bought from between the shafts of a pony trap when her owner drove up to the stud owned by the redoubtable Captain Machell. Isinglass grew to be an enormous three-year-old, appearing the more vast when his jockey, tiny Tom Loates, was aboard. Journalist Alexander Scott described Isinglass in his memoirs as 'the laziest horse I ever saw'. For all that he found enough energy to win the 2,000 Guineas and the St Leger as well as the Derby, beating poor Ravensbury into second place each time, and never by more than a length and a half. Isinglass won more than £57,000, a record which stood until the 1950s and Colonel McCalmont, who had in any case unexpectedly inherited an immense fortune from an Irish uncle, was well able to splash out on this memorial canvas which graced the house at Mount Juliet for nearly a century.

Before the Start, A Gentleman's Race EDGAR DEGAS

Jockeys in the Rain
EDGAR DEGAS

At the Racecourse HENRI DE TOULOUSE-LAUTREC

Riders on the Beach PAUL GAUGUIN

G. D. Giles (1857–1941) has produced a splendid record of that summer's day — the ground had been hard all year and the dust is flying as the stragglers come up the hill. The panoply of tents, the stands near the start — long vanished — are all recorded, and every face in the members' stand is a portrait. But the oddity is in the horses. The animals who are trailing in at the back — including the riderless horse — are painted with every sense of the new naturalism, but the leading pair are presented almost in caricature of the old style. It is as though both patron and artist had agreed that was the way Derby

Isinglass Wins the 1893 Derby
GODFREY GILES

winners were painted, had been painted and always should be painted, whatever the new-fangled ways — a view Giles at least was to cling to throughout his life.

At the turn of the century came Alfred Munnings (1878–1959), who was to become the most successful, and still the most valued, artist of this century. His painting is suffused with the Impressionist intoxication with colour and light — there is a sublime picture at his old house at Dedham of a white pony being led through a field of poppies, its flanks glowing with ruby reflections — yet it never abandoned conventional form and realism, and has proved as attractive in the saleroom as it became distasteful to his modernist critics. Munnings seems at his most sincere when painting plain and workaday horses and ponies, with the gypsies and labourers who bred them. But he also had a lasting fascination for the thoroughbred horse. It was oddly tentative, though, occupied coyly with the anticipation and the aftermath, with the rituals of preparation and obsequy, rarely with the climactic moments of racing itself. The rare moments when

Under Starter's Orders,
Newmarket
SIR ALFRED MUNNINGS

The Runaway SIR ALFRED MUNNINGS

Munnings did attempt some study of action, such as *The Runaway*, are invariably unconvincing. Yet his studies of the paddock at Epsom and Ascot, his marvellously atmospheric paintings of the runners against the lowering skyline on Newmarket Heath, are incomparable. The ferment as the field edge crabwise towards the starting tapes, jostling for advantage, poised always on the limit of control, is a splendid sight now erased by the mechanised starting stalls.

Munnings was bewitched by the theatricality and staging of racing. He wrote:

126

Study of Jockeys and Horses SIR ALFRED MUNNINGS

For me there is no paddock to equal that at Epsom. It is on the summit of a hill. Standing on the lower side one sees figures of horses and mounted jockeys silhouetted against the sky; others with their sheets being drawn off their backs; groups of trainers, owners, jockeys all in the bright light of an early English summer, a long white rail on the far side making a line through the picture — a scene for the artist. . . . I am watching shadows cast on the short grass, and the look of the sky and maybe the shape symmetry and lighting on a horse . . . wondering how light and how dark are the shade of Sir John Jarvis' colours.

Opposite
Her Majesty the Queen and
her horse Aureole
SIR ALFRED MUNNINGS

Going Out at Epsom
SIR ALFRED MUNNINGS

Munnings, in a long and versatile career, was always intrigued by racing, whether it was
the rumbustious exuberance of racing at St Buryan in Cornwall when he was joyously
embraced by the artists of the Newlyn School, Laura Knight — as fascinated as he was by
the gypsies — and her husband Harold, Stanhope Forbes and Lamorna Birch; or the later
immaculate and stately pictures which adorned his knighthood and his Presidency of the
Royal Academy. In Newlyn before the First World War Munnings was entranced by

Laura Knight. He wrote: 'In a low white-washed sail loft with a skylight Mrs Knight painted pictures which made the rest of us sit up. Here was a great artist who never ceased working. She possessed the energy of six; the studies for her larger pictures were wonderful. It was through her that I used china clay canvases.'

Indeed, almost fifty years on, that bright glorying in colour and light suffuses even the more solemn canvases of Munnings' later years. His picture of the Queen with her chestnut colt Aureole has a carefully composed and rather thoughtful gravity. It is Coronation year for the young sovereign and Aureole's part was to crown the season with a royal victory in the Derby. Cecil Boyd Rochfort, the Queen's trainer, and jockey Harry Carr stand respectfully aside while the horse is saddled up. Sadly, it was not to be. As Harry Carr said later: 'I am quite sure that Aureole had the misfortune to come up against one of the truly outstanding winners that afternoon at Epsom of the world's greatest race.' The winner was Pinza, Gordon Richards' only Derby winner. More than thirty years on, and still without a Derby winner, the Queen was to enquire wistfully of Slip Anchor's owner Lord Howard de Walden how he had achieved his Epsom success. 'You have to live as long as I have, Ma'am, and hope for the best,' he replied.

Photography had rescued horse painting from centuries of absurdity, and from renderings which provoke eternal derision — though many of the old artists, Sartorius, Wootton or Alken, did manage to invest great liveliness into these essentially stilted and unreal poses. The comprehension of the pattern of the galloping horse came at a time when the search for the sensation of speed had become an intoxicating quest which gripped innumerable areas of society. This was the age of the great railway contests with new locomotives and new lines vying with each other for records to Scotland and the west country. Transatlantic ships sought the blue riband, the America's Cup was launched. Even in racing there had been attempts to foster yearling races — short frantic dashes by unformed and immature stock.

Artists were inevitably seduced by this fever for speed, and gradually became aware that photography, which had initially seemed the ideal medium to capture momentum, was actually ill-equipped to convey those sensations which the public sought. It could merely stop the action in a single frame. It could not effectively convey movement, or grace, or that gamut of impressions which the spectator at live events garners through the human eye.

A number of painters became deeply interested in the challenge presented by the age of speed. The critic Oliver Beckett has republished the work of Lowes Dalbiac Luard (1872–1944), an artist who tackled this problem not only in his most original paintings, but also in a monograph entitled *Horses and Movement*, which he published in 1921. These were issues which artists who had not fled to the extremities of Impressionism or abstraction were trying to address in a number of fields. Duncan Grant's evanescent pictures of ballet dancers are equally concerned to fix that kaleidoscope of impressions which impresses the inward eye.

Luard pursued a musical analogy. 'Anyone who has watched a greyhound running must feel that the undulations of the animal, with their rhythmic series and culminating accents, are comparable to the run and rhythm of an air in music, whereas a momentary phase of the movement, such as is recorded in an instantaneous photograph, resembles a detached chord, and, like it, has little meaning out of its context.' He went on, 'Our perception of movement depends upon noting and comparing changes of shape, tone or colour, in a series of visual impressions, just as our sense of music depends upon the comparison of a series of momentary sounds.'

Luard then identified those aspects of what he called 'impressionistic realism' which

Overleaf
Steeplechase
LOWES DALBIAC LUARD

Harlequin and Colombine DUNCAN GRANT

help to convey movements — indistinctness, confusion, reduplication and apparent deformation. Above all he emphasised the importance of a rhythmic pattern to a picture.

These have been the tools which artists have used throughout this century in search of ways to paint the action on the racecourse. Lowes Luard's own pictures are remarkably successful in achieving these effects. His picture *Racing* produces an alarming reaction. With its long narrow format, the viewer almost expects the jockeys to disappear out of the picture at any moment, so vivid is the sensation of pace. The curves of the jockeys' backs, the arched tails, all packed together like waves on the sea, with the dense colours of the silks against a pastel background, combine to produce a vertiginous impact.

His picture of steeplechasers flowing over a fence fuses the movement of all the horses into one rounded whole — the sum of all the horses' action conveying the totality of one animal's leap and landing. Luard is remarkably effective in putting his theories on to canvas and his paintings are quite unlike those of any other racing artist.

The objectives he delineated have, however, been pursued by many of his successors. Most notable perhaps was the modest soldier artist, Gilbert Holiday (1879–1937). Artists from Alken onwards have been drawn to that decisive moment in the Derby when the field rounds Tattenham Corner to enter the straight. Some horses have become unbalanced coming down the hill, some are suddenly strapped for pace. The turn is brutally sharp and some are carried wide and far towards the grandstand rails. Any jockey who still harbours any hope of victory must now fight for his position. It is a thunderous moment with a huge crowd invariably on the rails as the race finally unfolds. Holiday's 1933 pastel and watercolour, set against the looming crowd and the distant stands, plunges into the maelstrom. There are horses skidding round the extremity of the turn, laggards being rousted up at the back, a dark bay being checked for room in the turmoil of the pack. The picture seems to shout with noise as well as colour.

Holiday was a superb draughtsman, but with great vigour of expression. He could paint horses from any angle and the effects of action and movement flow through his paintings even when as tranquil a metaphor as a rainbow is arching over his painting of the mêlée at a start.

Holiday, like his contemporary Adrian Jones, was held in high esteem by his brother officers, and much of his work is in the private possession of regimental messes. He was

Top
Racing
LOWES DALBIAC LUARD

Bottom
Rainbow Start, Ascot
GILBERT HOLIDAY

Secretariat JOHN SKEAPING

also in great demand as an illustrator, and became a brave and intrepid war artist. His career was cut sadly short. In 1932 he had a bad fall while out hunting with the Woolwich drag hounds. He was paralysed and five years later died of pneumonia. His book *Horses and Soldiers* was published posthumously.

Most notable of his successors perhaps has been John Skeaping (1901–80). Skeaping freely admitted that the best part of his health, wealth and happiness came from the racing scene. He made some splendid portrait bronzes, including life-size evocations of Hyperion and Brigadier Gerard, and the set of four horses in a driving finish which are displayed outside the weighing room at Newmarket. Skeaping's bronze of Secretariat is a supreme evocation of the power of the thoroughbred, hurtling out in that explosion of speed which produced unprecedented victories — 60 lengths in the 1973 Belmont Stakes.

Modern physiology and photography may have permitted an understanding of how the racehorse runs, yet that understanding only reinforces our awe. The horse is taking six

Previous page
Tattenham Corner
GILBERT HOLIDAY

tons of force on his pastern bones as he puts each foot down. His heart surges to ten times its normal rate. His lungs are extracting a litre of oxygen with every stride. Bursting out of the starting stalls he can accelerate from a standstill to 50 miles an hour in two and a half seconds, a matter of half a dozen strides. 'The racehorse is designed by God to explode into a machine that defies physiology,' said Dr George Pratt, the veterinarian at the Massachusetts Institute of Technology.

Skeaping's most original work, however, is his painting of action on the racecourse, sublime executions of Luard's principles, especially his pictures of racing in America. From the instant the handlers release the bridles and the starting stalls clang open, American racing is full-blooded, not tactical in the European style. Across the nation the racegoer can cherish in confident anticipation the critical moment when, as celebrated race caller Dave Johnson invariably tells it, 'they come spinning out of the turn'. It is in those moments of elation that the race is so often won — or cast away. Only those who survive that centrifugal force can claim their place in the final dash along the stretch to the wire. The resolution is swift, straightforward, devoid of subterfuge.

These are animals which have been trained relentlessly against the stop watch, 'breezed' in the jargon for all-out time-trials. There is no place for the dubious limb or suspect stamina. There is an unremitting intensity to all American racing.

Skeaping's pastels and gouaches vibrate with the abrupt excitement of the dirt and the Turf — American style. Even his English pictures are touched by that same dynamism. 'The Race', a gouache from 1974, is a brilliant assault on the senses. Three horses in frantic rivalry are leaning round a left-hand turn. Skeaping can be a painstaking draughtsman, but these are pure impressions: from close-up a blur of paint; from a pace or two away the most splendid portrayal of high-blooded action. In bronze, Skeaping is an artist of grace and composure. On paper and canvas he captures the high moments of the race track as though the colours themselves were blended with adrenalin.

There is a splendid pastel, 'Last Furlong', which shows just one horse, unthreatened by any rival, but flat for the line, the tail bannered, the jockey crouched superbly on the neck like Angel Cordero at his finest. Skeaping's pastels on grey paper, economical in colour, have a restrained and uncluttered quality which is appealing. But it is his dramatic gouaches which perhaps have captured the excitements of modern racing beyond compare.

The Race – Six Furlongs
JOHN SKEAPING

Racing USA JOHN SKEAPING

Half a Length GRAHAM ISOM

Three Racehorses MIRJAM VERHOEFF

Skeaping set a tone in the post-war years which has been followed by the best of the young artists. Their pictures command as acute an involvement as the most committed racegoer could demand. There is nothing detached here. Graham Isom's *Half a Length* is painted from the point of view of the spectator on the rails. Looking up, there is a tremendous impression of the looming bulk and power of the mature racehorse — not only the pace but the daunting impulsion as the jockey kneels into the withers. This is the long, utterly straight and flat final four furlongs at York — the scene of Roberto's supernatural defeat of Brigadier Gerard in 1972, the arena for some of the epic sprint races of recent times, where the great mare Soba caught Scarrowmanwick on the line; where Sharpo seemed invincible, and Never So Bold was so heroic on his fragile limbs. From the five-furlong start there is scarcely an inch of deviation to the finish and not an ounce of quarter to be given. Isom's portrait of Padrong, enviably muscled, all out under Lester Piggott to hold the challenge of Greville Starkey on Lucky Sovereign, is a paean to the modern thoroughbred in action.

Mirjam Verhoeff's spare impressionistic style, shorn of irrelevant background and detail, in her large study *Three Racehorses* focuses on the moment when the starters burst on to the track, all three gathered like quarter-horses for the sudden acceleration. Drawn in muted pastel on grey paper, her pictures distil the frenetic moments when races are decided. These modern painters aim to capture the thrill of sinewed speed which seduces all horsemen. When they succeed, the finest fleeting moments of the track can live forever.

Overleaf
Races at Longchamp
EDOUARD MANET

VI
Racing International

The racing scene has flourished around the world in the last two centuries, and racing is followed as avidly in the Orient as in Europe or South America, has survived the disapproval of Marxist-Leninism in the Soviet Union, and outlasted its colonial founders in India and Africa. The centrepieces of world racing, beyond the old classics in England and America, are now the Prix de l'Arc de Triomphe in Paris and the Breeders' Cup Day and International races in the United States, when millions of dollars are offered in prize money.

An Arc day at Longchamp in the 1980s offers a cameo of this gilded global caravan. The race is over. Back down the course towards the winner's enclosure, in line like a sovereign's escort, come the three horses of Daniel Wildenstein. Sagace has passed the post first. Wildenstein, father and son together, march beaming forward. Their young trainer Patrick Biancone bustles behind, aide-de-camp. Two million francs await the winner. Among the defeated are the Aga Khan, Lord Weinstock, Lord Tavistock, Robert Sangster, and Sheik Abdullah of Dubai. Short of altering the destiny of nations, the moment is as near a Roman triumph as mortal men can strive for.

Then the dreadful sound of a hooter disturbs the tumult. The horrible apprehension of losing the race after all dawns on the faces of the two Wildensteins — shortly to be confirmed as the objection is sustained. Biancone, in true Gallic fashion, is simply furious. The crowd pelt and berate all things English; the horse, Rainbow Quest, who has been given the race; the jockey, though he's Irish; the owner, though he's Arab.

The next month, many of these horses are half a world away in Laurel, Maryland for the Washington International. The November gloom gives small encouragement to dreams of glory. Few spectators bother to leave their seats to watch the horses saddled. Horses here have numbers to be played, not names to be conjured with. But huddled in

La Llegada
VINCENTE FORTE

the centre of Laurel's old khaki barn, nimbly avoiding the flying feet, dodging puddles, many of the actors from Longchamp have gathered again. Lord Weinstock has made the trip, and the Marchioness of Tavistock. The Marquesa Incisa della Rochetta's colt Iades is running. This time the blue blood of America has staked a claim. Hall of Fame trainer Woodford C. Stephens runs Crème Fraîche, the Belmont winner. Lester Piggott was there too, riding his last race on American soil, for the American Ambassador to France, William Kazan. The race was straightforward. Vanlandingham won, post to wire, for America.

For the few who cared there was a last sight of Piggott, trailing unnoticed across the boardwalk, being shouldered into the slop of the dirt track by the troop of track stewards escorting Eva Gabor and Merv Griffin across to present the trophies. Of all the farewells, this last in America was the loneliest as the slight figure, almost unrecognisable in the livery of mud and dirt which distinguishes American losers, left the track for the plane to Europe. While the track's new owner was saying Hello to Mom over the loudspeaker as the stars presented the prizes, Piggott disappeared, unregarded. Yet it was here that he had won with perhaps his greatest horse, Sir Ivor, in 1968, with Karabas the next year, and then in 1980 with Argument. At Laurel, too, there had been no jockey like him.

For thirty years the management of Laurel and John D. Schapiro in particular had felt the need to capture on canvas the fleeting moments of glory. His tastes ran to modernism. Aguina and Agurra were commissioned, and Vincente Forte asked to paint the great mural celebrating three International winners from the heady days when international racing was Schapiro's personal dream. Forte's *La Llegada* (The Finish) is a huge Braque-like work, the angular shadows and perspectives reflecting the sharp light of sundown on the brighter days at Laurel. The horses are masked in blinkers, but the figures of both horses and jockeys are rounded, ripe with life against the austere cubist fawns and browns of the track itself. This is an idealised race, impossible on this earth, between three great winners of the International.

On the other side of America, Hollywood Park, scene of one of the greatest races of the 1980s, the Breeders' Cup match when the 1987 Kentucky Derby winner Alysheba went down by a head to Ferdinand, the victor of the previous year, hosts a panorama of shrieking modernity. Singapore Airlines, with Air France in pursuit, are yawning

Muddy Trip at
Hollywood Park
CELESTE SUSANY

alarmingly almost on to the club house bend. Delta, American, United, wheels down, flaps down and lined up on the other runway at Los Angeles International Airport, seem in fact all set to put down on the Hollywood Park home turn. A full bright orange moon is slotted with slide rule precision atop the back stretch. The slab of floodlighting runs the vast length of the stand. Giant screens flicker messages and replays in glaring yellow, blue and orange neon. Electric numbers run the whole length of the stretch, constantly changing, given no peace by the computers feeding win, show, place, exacta. Phalanxes of bright blue tractors manicure the track and haul the yellow starting gates into position.

The glistening glass of the Turf Club, water cascading tastefully down the walls of the escalator well, seems distant and remote — the glass front keeping the air conditioning in, and the atmosphere of the track out. The Chicago Bears and Michigan are colliding on every other TV screen. It is a strange environment in which to try the mettle of the thoroughbred horse — but a perfect place to gamble on the outcome, and the artists of California have found it fertile ground for the bright and fevered painting which appeals in the West.

Racing round the world is, indeed, an urban sport: Moonee Valley in the middle of a suburban housing estate in Melbourne, Australia; the Kentucky Derby track down the side streets of Louisville; the Aintree Grand National course at the back of a chemical and rayon factory.

But the most spectacular tracks are in the Orient. Roy Miller's picture of night racing at Happy Valley in Hong Kong is a silvered evocation of racing in the vast arena at the heart of one of the world's most stunning cities. A hundred blocks or more of apartments, each fifty stories high, turn the Valley into an awesome canyon, the pure jewelled green turf its centrepiece — the highways on stilts snaking up through the buildings in the background; neon everywhere, unblinking in accordance with regulations, and the more persistent for that. Yet in the midst of this clattering city, it is the sounds of Happy Valley which linger: the sigh of satisfaction from a Chinese crowd when the starting gates open and the fabulous totalisator pool is in play, the thunder of hoofs as the horses pass almost directly below the seven-tier stands, the soft and overwhelming collective moan when a favourite is disqualified.

Sha Tin, Hong Kong's new course over on the mainland, is probably the most modern

Night Racing at Happy Valley ROY MILLER

and luxurious racecourse in the world, but Happy Valley at night in the last days of empire, such an extraordinary confluence of Chinese and English interests and excitements, is the most exhilarating place for horsemen in the whole of Asia.

But the track which perhaps offers the most encouragement is the Moscow Hippodrome. In the bitter cold of a winter's afternoon a regular crowd of a few hundred make their way each Sunday to the stadium. It is crumbling now, but the track was constructed in the style of a colosseum. There are totalisator gambling windows and men with fistfuls of rouble tickets. The track itself is packed snow, with both flat racing and trotting with sledges. The highlight of the afternoon, two troika teams of three horses each, careering their sledges round the tight turns, must be the nearest sight left on earth to the scenes millennia ago in the old Roman Colosseum.

These Russian horsemen have kept the faith through the darkest days of Communism. The oppressive, puritan philosophy of Lenin and Stalin disapproved of gambling, as of so many popular pastimes. Horsemen disappeared suddenly off the streets and into the prisons and the camps. Racing was starved of all publicity. To this day, many Muscovites do not know that the Hippodrome is still active. Yet the trainers and the jockeys, conscripted, like all other workers, from the private farms and stables into state employment, managed to keep the sport alive. Even after the war, when large areas of the Soviet Union were literally starving, the horsemen kept racing.

One of the leading Russian jockeys, Nikolai Nasibov, described the difficulties they faced: 'The riding hall was small. In fact it was an old aircraft hangar. You could manage dressage and jumping in it, but training a racing stallion was another matter. I would get the stallion up into a gallop with the trainer yelling "Faster". It would often end up in a fall. Not that I would be thrown out of the saddle, but I would fall with the horse.'

Not far from the Moscow Hippodrome is an extraordinary and unknown treasure house, which explains the deep roots of this stoic tradition: the Moscow Museum of Horsebreeding. Few westerners have ever entered the portals of this old house on a quiet tree-lined suburban street. Inside is to be found probably the most extraordinary display of equestrian art in the world. The rooms are filled with hundreds of paintings, some of them enormous, sweeping studies. But most striking of all is their quality. In particular there are over two hundred pictures by N. G. Sverchkoff (1817–98), who was an art professor in Moscow. Their impact is quite stunning. Exquisitely executed, bursting with life, the colours fresh as the day they were painted, it is not hyperbole to suggest that Sverchkoff was one of the greatest talents in equestrian art.

The cultural isolation of Russia since the Revolution obscures the memory that Moscow and St Petersburg were an integral part of European artistic life until the curtain came down so abruptly in 1917. Just before the First World War the English Derby winners Minoru and Aboyeur were exported to Russia, only to disappear in the maelstrom. But there had been a strong horse trade with Russia well before the Moscow racecourse opened in 1834.

The Druid recalls Mr Kirby of York: 'This wonderful old man first set foot at Cronstadt (St Petersburg) in 1791, when he was little more than twenty-one, in charge of a string of horses which a speculative Market Weighton brewer sent out at a venture.'

Grey Horse
N. G. SVERCHKOFF

Kirby only lost one horse at sea in sixty years of voyaging to Russia, yet ironically lost fourteen drowned in one night when the River Neva burst its banks and flooded Kirby's stables at St Petersburg. In the turbulent politics of the time, Kirby once only got home by hitching a lift on Nelson's flagship in the Baltic. But he was invariably welcome at the Winter Palace, selling Czar Nicholas the St Leger winner Van Tromp for 2,000 guineas and General Chasse for 2,250 guineas.

He was selling a stallion called Brough and a load of mares to Count Koutightsoff when that gentleman disappeared in order to cut the throat of the Emperor Paul. Kirby joined the privileged crowd who viewed the imperial body just where it fell and then went out to visit the Count, who was already under arrest at his house. The Count coolly offered to sell the stallion back for the £500 which he had paid for the whole draft.

In this turbulent atmosphere there was a great demand for paintings. Sverchkoff became the best-known artist of his day, producing hunting, troika and forest scenes, as

Racer
N. G. SVERCHKOFF

156

well as many racing pictures. He came to Paris in 1863 to exhibit at the Paris Exhibition, and then went on to London for a one-man show where forty of his paintings were sold.

Another of the outstanding artists to be seen at the Museum of Horsebreeding is X. Shtephek. It was in Russia on the stud farms of Count Orlov-Chesmensky that the famous Orlov trotters were bred from the Arab stallion Smetanka, imported from Turkey in 1776, a venture that was as momentous for the breeding of trotting horses as the arrival of the Darley Arabian for thoroughbreds. Count Orlov would never sell stallions from his stud, gelding every colt foal that he allowed out, but the blood got out through a faithless stableman. Kholstomer, about whom Tolstoy wrote, and who was the fastest trotter of the nineteenth century in Russia, was supposed to be gelded. But he was surreptitiously put to a mare before the knife struck. The result was Satin, from whose line came Bull Calf, another legendary trotter.

The museum has other notable artists, altogether a testament to the most vigorous

The Grey, Gallant
X. SHTEPHEK

tradition of equestrian painting, which has effectively been forgotten by Western connoisseurs. In the Soviet Union it was only preserved by a provincial trainer from Prilepsk, Y. I. Butovich, who collected the paintings that form the core of this astonishing collection.

The Russians have had some outstanding horses in modern times, among them Anilin, who won the Europe Cup in 1965, 1966, and 1967 in Cologne, and ran in the Washington International in Laurel, Maryland. In 1989 a team of Orlov trotters went to the Meadowlands in New York and performed respectably. But the dream remains distant of a horse to come out of the purdah of seventy years of revolution, privation and state horse farms and reassert on the racecourses of the West the powerful blood which was exported to Russia over a period of a century and more.

As it happens the General Chasse who was sold to the Czar by Kirby was the subject of one of John Ferneley's pictures when he was the property of the Midlands baronet Sir James Boswell. Ferneley (1782–1860) had a great talent for portraying the bloom of a racehorse in its full fitness, the highlights gleaming on the coat, but invariably, it seems, with some exaggeration of the small head and neck so prized by thoroughbred owners in the first century after the foundation Arabs arrived in England.

He also had a great facility for conveying a relaxed and easy charm in his pictures. General Chasse looks supple and calm in this picture, and his trainer stands casually with hand on hip. The jockey, J. Holmes, strolling into the picture, is wearing Boswell's colours, and the setting is Liverpool racecourse before the era of the Grand National, where General Chasse won the 1835 Liverpool St Leger. He won twenty races including the 1837 Chester Cup, or the Tradesmen's Cup as it was then known, carrying 9 stone 7 lb, the largest weight borne to victory there at that time.

Ferneley, the son of a Leicestershire wheelwright, flourished principally among the hunting men of Melton and the Quorn, but he also travelled and worked extensively in Ireland, in Yorkshire and in London. His daughter Sarah and his two sons, John junior and Claude Lorraine Ferneley, were all notable painters, but without quite the quality of their father. Ferneley's patrons are known about in great detail as his account books survived virtually intact and were edited by Major Guy Paget.

General Chasse JOHN FERNELEY

VII
Jockeys

Jockeys have always been the object of venom or veneration, according to whether they delivered the desired result to owners and betting men. From the Chifneys through Fred Archer to Steve Donoghue and Lester Piggott, they have been figures as well known as any on the racing scene. Their portraits have been painted, by Herring and Marshall, but frequently they are seen, ill-defined, in the saddle, an ancillary to the star of the picture, the horse. Few artists have attempted to reflect the conflicts and tensions of the jockey's life.

John Lavery (1856–1941), Irishman by birth, Scotsman by adoption into the Glasgow School, acquired a knighthood and a fortune as perhaps the most fashionable of Victorian portrait painters. Yet in his maturer years, almost as a private vice, he indulged a fascination with the backstage scenes of racing. Going to the Epsom Derby of 1924, he gave us not the spotlit drama of Sansovino winning the race in an unprecedented quagmire for the Earl of Derby, but Tommy Weston weighing in after the race amid a throng of excited 'connections'.

And in *A Jockeys' Changing Room* — painted slanting away from us as though from a cupboard in the corner — Lavery captures superbly the bustle and tension of the weighing room, the jockeys thrown together yet strangely isolated, the brightness of the silks, fragile as butterflies in the long dark chamber. One young man, shirtless, apprehensive, stands gazing out of the high windows. There is fellow feeling here, but no camaraderie. In the coming contest, victory for one is defeat for all the rest. Lavery has grasped remarkably well this private scene. Owners and trainers are not welcome. The jostle of press and tout remains beyond the door. The horses have yet to reach the paddock. The public drama is still a while off, but this dim antechamber is an evocative prologue, recorded by an artist who spent much of his time portraying the great and the self-important, but who in racing happily showed little interest in the grander show.

Issues of honour and loyalty between jockeys, owners, trainers, and stable staff have stirred the racing world since the earliest days. Two centuries ago the Prince of Wales abandoned Newmarket forever rather than desert his jockey Sam Chifney.

A Jockeys' Changing Room
SIR JOHN LAVERY

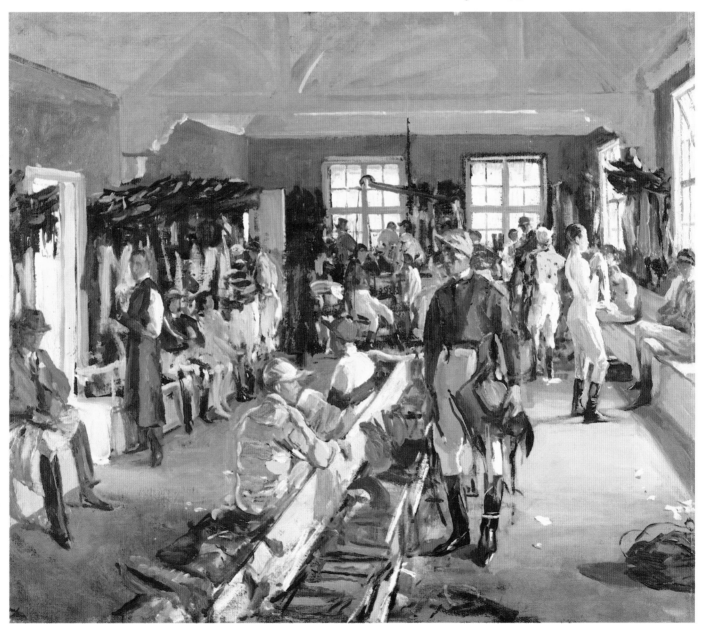

At Doncaster on St Leger Day in 1984 the cauldron was bubbling again. Commanche Run, a handsome bay son of Run the Gantlet, had won a string of races in England ridden by the American jockey Darrell McHargue. McHargue, tough and hard driving in the saddle but open-hearted and charming out of it, had endeared himself to the English racing public in a summer when he had ridden fifty winners. He had ridden Commanche Run well. There was no possible cause for criticism. Then, two days before the St Leger, and against the most strenuous protests of trainer Luca Cumani, owner Ivan Allan

'jocked off' McHargue and asked Lester Piggott to ride instead. Piggott accepted. McHargue, in disgust, flew back to America.

It was totally in character. Twenty years before, Piggott had scandalised the English racing world by spurning the employer who had given him classic victories, Noel Murless, to rampage as a freelance through the traditional arrangements of commitment and continuity which characterised English racing. And by the autumn of 1984 Piggott had won the same number of classic victories as Frank Buckle had notched up a century

The Weighing Room
PETER BIEGEL

Lester Piggott
RAYMOND SKIPP

and a half before. His ambition, as he approached his forty-ninth birthday and his final season, was palpable. The means were impugned on all sides. There was great sympathy for McHargue.

But another loyalty has always run through the fabric of racing — the duty to do the best by the horse itself. The desire to allow, indeed to encourage the horse to fulfil its highest potential is a thread, mingled though it may be in a skein of ambition, greed, and pride, which has justified decisions that might otherwise have attracted only obloquy.

The St Leger of 1984 was to offer a text. Piggott had already won seven St Legers, though he had also suffered some setbacks, notably seven years before when, riding the dual Arc de Triomphe winner Alleged, he was defeated by the Queen's great mare Dunfermline. 'Thanks to Lester, she had two pacemakers,' muttered Alleged's trainer Vincent O'Brien.

There are still five furlongs to go when the runners enter the relentless straight at Doncaster. And there were more than two left when Commanche Run struck the front. Almost immediately he was tackled by Shernazar, and then, still two furlongs out, by the Aga Khan's colt Baynoun. All the way down in front of the stands the two ran straight as a die. It seemed inevitable that Baynoun, brought on the outside by Steve Cauthen, would prevail. For that whole desperate quarter of a mile Commanche Run was never more than half a length in front. It seemed his strength could not possibly last. Yet Piggott, supernatural that day, spurning the whip, hardly moving, somehow held the horse together throughout that long struggle, to win by a neck.

The sustained roar of the Doncaster crowd, showed recognition not only of a great occasion in racing history, Piggott's classic record, and an epic battle, but also of the fact that no other jockey alive could have written the name of Commanche Run on the St Leger roll in the face of Baynoun's dynamic challenge. The greatest loyalty, to the horse, had to some extent overwhelmed regret at all that had gone before.

VIII
Trotting

Trotting is the chariot racing of modern times. Seeing the sulkies with their gossamer wheels shimmering towards a bend, there is always the premonition of disaster. The funneling of horses, outfits, drivers, into the final straight seems impossible. Sometimes the worst happens, and there is a sudden collision of man, horseflesh, metal and the frightening confusion of tack and harness which confines the trotting horse. But on the whole teams stay upright and compete in the eerie, muted straining of trotting's final dash for the line. For there is an ethereal quality to trotting. No thunder of galloping hoofs, only the creak of the elaborate harness and the crack of the long whips. The surge of the best horses, emphasised by the spinning wheels, often seems supernatural. The system of handicapping by distance rather than by weight produces apparently prodigious feats of overtaking to excite the watchers in the stand.

Trotting has for a century or more been the most popular form of racing in France and America. In the last few years it has been challenged in both countries by the glamour of thoroughbred racing, but its attraction as a spectator sport and above all a gambling event is undiminished. Trotting is made for gambling. The horses run all the time, week in, week out, for years on end. The drivers last long enough to make Willie Shoemaker seem young. The tracks scarcely vary. The gambler can feel that at least some of the miasma of uncertainty which confronts him in any horse race has been contained. In return sums are wagered at Meadowlands and Vincennes which make Aqueduct and Longchamp seem beggarly.

Trotting developed in the United States as the supreme national sport of the nineteenth century, immortalised in the prolific output of the New York lithographers, Currier and Ives. For fifty years they brought the work of America's foremost artists to an enormous public through their prints, focusing on the celebrated event, the dramatic incident, the epic heroes of a momentous half century. When Nathaniel Currier was selling his first popular work — of the burning of the *Lexington* in Long Island Sound in 1840 — Lewis and Clark still had not set off from St Louis for the first crossing of the continent. By 1895, when James Ives died, the partners had chronicled the rise of the most dynamic society in the world. They had lionised Lincoln and Grant as the North's champions in the Civil War, they had sustained Frederic Remington's visions of the myths and glories of the opening up of the West, and they had warmed America's image of itself as a rustic idyll of hearth and farm. And, born of personal enthusiasm, and a sense of the public's avid appetite, they had raised the sport of trotting racing to its zenith.

Currier and Ives produced more than 650 prints of trotters and trotting racing in the half century up to 1895. They were the arbiters of glory; their verdict apotheosised the Kings and Queens of the Turf; and their taste for drama and excitement shaped the exaggerated, breathless, and high-flown style which gives much American racing art such a memorable and instant impact.

Nicholas Winfield Scott Leighton (1849–98) was the last and most outstanding of Currier and Ives' trotting artists. A native of Maine, he established a studio in Boston where critics admired the accuracy and empathy of his horse painting. Yet by the time he painted the portrait of St Julien, he had refined the features which were the stamp of the Currier and Ives artists. Philip Pines, conservator of so much of their work, has defined them: 'The animals' elongated bodies, flaring nostrils, prominent flashing eyes and outstretched legs, gave the effect the lithographers wanted.' St Julien was the world record holder in 1880. Like so many trotting heroes he had had the humblest of beginnings, pulling a milk cart to the railway station in Orange County, New York, before being bought out of the East and taken to California by the famous driver Orrin Hickok. He broke the world record there at Oakland before being brought back East again to Rochester and Hartford to prove twice more that it was no accident.

From the beginning, trotting had been the people's sport of America, born as it was out of natural rivalry on the paths and roadways of town and countryside. Horses were the only means of travel and the continent soon evolved its own distinctive breed, the Narragansett pacer which could cover long distances at speed and in comfort. The pacer's gait, moving both legs on one side and then both on the other, produced an easy if rather nautical-looking rolling stride, which made for the most relaxed ride. Trotters, using diagonally opposite legs, proved to be much more suited to pulling the light carts which developed for the new roads.

166

St Julien NICHOLAS WINFIELD SCOTT LEIGHTON

Thomas Worth's comic confection for Currier and Ives, *Coming From the Trot*, painted in 1869, with patrons returning in their four-wheelers from the Union Course on Long Island past Hiram Woodruff's famous roadhouse, suggests all the possibilities and pitfalls which made trotting so immensely popular. As the network of roads and highways grew across first the Eastern seaboard and, later, the Western and Midwestern states, the horse with a carriage became the universal transport. A man of quite modest means could and did aspire to own a pony and trap. Once on the road, he was ready to challenge any man. Worth's picture celebrates that importunate urge which must have overtaken almost every journeyman on America's roads to try his set against a fellow traveller. These impromptu 'brushes' on the highway were by all accounts a constant feature of life on the road, especially where high days, holidays, or social imbibing had injected a competitive spirit into the horsemen of the day. There were well known stretches, straight and true, like Third Avenue and Harlem Lane in New York, where contests were arranged, or where young bloods loitered waiting the chance to race. Worth's picture of 'devil take the hindmost' rivalry, one participant catapulted on to his horse while his carriage breaks up behind, another clearly destined to be deposited in the dirt while his pair of chestnuts bolts away, reflects the uproarious, carefree and plain hazardous joyracing which made sedate travellers tremble, but excited men of every class. Men like Robert Bonner and William Vanderbilt could pay fortunes for a good trotter or pacer, but many a champion was bought for a handful of dollars and driven on the road long before it reached the track. Brown Hal, the champion of 1889, was bought as a foal for just $56 and 50 cents.

Thomas Worth (1834–1917) was a New Yorker from Greenwich Village. He was a great friend of James Ives and his constant companion at the trotting tracks, but never an employee. Though he was an excellent draughtsman and produced some fine portraits such as that of the chestnut mare Music, it was his comic gifts which made his fortune. He was the Rowlandson of his day. *Coming From the Trot* is full of amusement at the pratfalls and posturings of the drivers, with urinating layabouts in the background, and ladies peeking from behind upstairs curtains. But it was the unapologetic cartoons which proved supremely popular. Some of his so-called 'Darktown comics' sold 70,000 copies or more.

Coming From the Trot THOMAS WORTH

The Sealskin Brigade NICHOLAS WINFIELD SCOTT LEIGHTON

Robert Bonner, a New York publisher, and William Vanderbilt both bought the most famous and expensive trotters principally to drive themselves in showdowns on the road against their peers, rather than to race them on the track. Scott Leighton's great picture *The Sealskin Brigade* portrays some of these wealthy participants in a winter 'brush' with trotters and sleighs on Seventh Avenue, New York, with the Macomb's Dam Bridge in the background. It was painted for A. W. Richmond who is seen with the grey trotter Hopeful. Vanderbilt, with the mutton chop whiskers, is driving Maud S. outside the grey. Robert Bonner, in the high silk hat, is driving the pair. The others are notable enough figures. Foster, patriarch of the Dewey family, is driving Richard on Bonner's inside. Leighton has painted the world record holder St Julien again, unflatteringly squeezed in at the back behind Dewey, with Orrin Hickok driving. Frank Work with Edward Swiveler is tucked in behind Vanderbilt.

This is elevated company, and not only in Wall Street terms. Hopeful, a gelding who had been owned by a Mr Gillender, had won all the Grand Circuit races — the classic series — in 1878 and held a mile record of 2 minutes 14¾ seconds. Maud S., bought as a yearling for $250 in Kentucky in 1875, had become world champion by 1881, trotting a mile in 2 minutes 10¼ seconds at Rochester, New York. In the grandiose fashion of the time, she was later sold by Vanderbilt to Bonner for $40,000, and lowered the world record for the seventh time in 1885 to 2 minutes 8¾ seconds at Cleveland, Ohio.

Scott Leighton's large and luxurious picture, as silky a sheen to the sealskin cloaks and hats as to the high quality horseflesh, captures an age of wagers and private challenges which provided unmatched public spectacle for the strollers and citizens of New York.

Henry Cross's (1837–1918) subscription picture of the Old Union racecourse in New York in 1884 brings together many of the great characters of trotting racing in its golden age, though some of the identities have been misattributed. The man in cap and beard leaning on the rail holding a whip cannot be Hiram Woodruff — he had been dead sixteen years — but the man in the blue cap probably is Dan Mace. Dan and Benny Mace were great trainers and drivers of the era, producing the likes of Hopeful and also turning out some noteworthy young drivers like W. H. 'Knapsack' McCarthy. Immediately behind him in a silk hat and holding a crop is John Morrisey, one of the founders of the Saratoga track and sometime New York Senator, bookmaker and heavyweight champion

The Old Union Course, 1884
HENRY CROSS

of the world. There is a Vanderbilt there — Commodore Cornelius — Colonel Crosby and enough New York swells to show how fashionable as well as popular trotting had become. The race itself is being won by Grey Eddy, driven by Harry Jones, from Sim Hooglana's True John.

The first special trotting track in America was laid out at Hunting Park, Philadelphia,

in 1829, and R. S. Hillman's delightful primitive picture of a race there is the earliest known painting of American trotting. It is full of fascination, with the covered wagons parked at the side, and the contestants already decked out at this era in racing silks and caps. There is an impressively large crowd and no fewer than three grandstands, with most of the spectators inside the sand track. Ridden trotters were the more popular in

The First Trotting Race
R. S. HILLMAN

173

that era before adequate roads, and the horses were suitably enduring. In this race, won by Dread, there were four three-mile heats, and the second horse, Topgallant, was twenty-four years old! A curiosity of the race was that one of the riders, George Woodruff, rode three different horses, including Topgallant, in three heats. Woodruff was the first recorded trotting trainer and rider in a family which was to dominate American trotting for much of the century. His nephew Hiram Woodruff trained and drove many champions and wrote the book *The Trotting Horse of America*, which is the source of much of our knowledge of early trotting racing.

Topgallant has a unique place in the history of trotting. He was already sixteen years old when a wealthy enthusiast called Harry Costar recruited him for a specially arranged match at the Union course on Long Island, on the day that the thoroughbred track was staging the famous match between Eclipse and Fashion. Sixty thousand spectators had their first intimation that trotting could rival thoroughbred racing as a spectator attraction, as Topgallant beat Costar's own horse Betsy Baker. For the next eight years Topgallant, who had acquired his strength and stamina pulling hackney cabs, raced consistently along the East Coast including many jousts with the celebrated horse Whalebone. In one match at Hunting Park against Whalebone, Topgallant, by then twenty-two years old, averaged under three minutes per mile for sixteen miles, ridden by the same George Woodruff. Trotting racing under saddle is a rare sight these days, too contained and rarified a taste perhaps for spectators who have never sat a horse themselves, and banished to gymkhanas and county fairs.

From the earliest era, trotting enthusiasts have been obsessed by time to an extent unknown in thoroughbred racing. Indeed 'the great fountainhead of trotting speed' (as the *Horse Review* put it in 1886), William Rysdyk's Hambletonian, was only ever tried against the clock — he trotted a mile in 2 minutes 48½ seconds as a three-year-old — and was never trained for racing.

J. H. Wright's picture of him in 1865 with his owner, reproduced as one of Currier and Ives' most majestic prints, shows the superb conformation, beautifully balanced, mighty shoulders, and powerful quarters which attracted mare owners before he was three years old. One of the foals of Hambletonian's first covering season as a two-year-old turned out to be another legendary sire, Alexander's Abdallah.

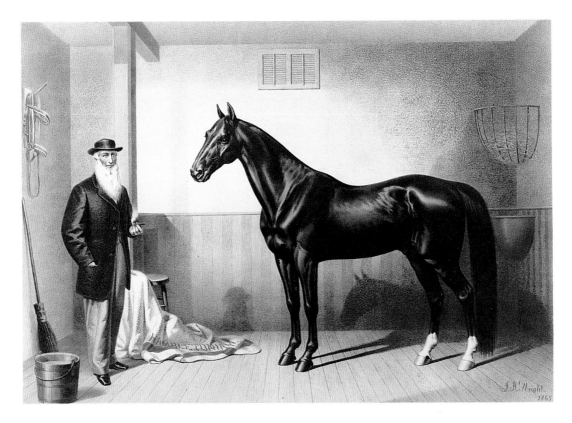

Hambletonian J. H. WRIGHT

If there is an air of calm confidence and determination about Wright's portrayal of Hambletonian's owner, it is amply merited. William Rysdyk was pinched for money in the summer of 1851, when Hambletonian was two, and offered him up for sale by auction at his home in Chester, New York. There was no bid. But afterwards when a pair of leading horsemen of the day, John Minchin and George Payne, thought to buy him, Rysdyk would not take less than $1,000. Later, before anyone really knew his worth, Robert Bonner offered $20,000 for him. Rysdyk, still at the time a poor man, refused again. His stubbornness gained sumptuous reward. Hambletonian's service fee, $25 in 1852, had reached $50 by 1866. He died ten years and a thousand mares later, to be suitably memorialised in granite beside Hambletonian Avenue in Chester.

Hambletonian's most famous son, Dexter, is known not only for his victories, but for his times: 2 minutes 31¼ when he was first tried over a mile with a sulky behind him at five years old; four years on, a world record of 2 minutes 17¼, after the same Robert Bonner had bought him for $35,000.

Trotting records, unlike thoroughbred records, have been consistently lowered through the years. There is no doubt that this has been substantially due to astute breeding and refined training methods, as well as improved surfaces. But with trotting, technology offers opportunities not available to thoroughbred racers. When the Italian cyclists appeared at the Los Angeles Olympics with solid-wheeled racing bikes, apparently offering marginally reduced drag and increased speed, and then proceeded to sweep the board, the new fashion was rapidly adapted for trotting sulkies.

Trotting men have constantly sought to gain an edge with better carriages. Though the chariots of ancient times were two-wheeled, the early racing carriage of modern days was a four-wheeled wagon. By the time that track racing evolved, the characteristic sulky with two high wheels, finely fashioned with slender spokes, had become the dominant vehicle. The wheels became progressively smaller so that by the end of the century the typical bicycle wheel carried most racing drivers. There has been an unending search for refinements, many of which have been tried only to be outlawed. A windshield pulled by a thoroughbred galloper was tried in 1903 at Yonkers raceway in an attempt to lower the world record with a pacer called Prince Alert. He succeeded, but the run was officially disqualified. In the 1970s there were experiments with single, central shaft sulkies in an attempt to reduce wind resistance. These too were soon banished from the tracks. Oddly, in contrast to thoroughbred racing, the weight and indeed sheer bulk of the driver as added wind resistance has rarely been seen as of much account, skill and experience often residing in positively portly shapes on the trotting track.

The earliest recorded trotting races in both England and America were races against time. The English race took place on Newmarket Heath on 29 August 1750. It was depicted in a celebrated picture commissioned from James Seymour by one of the sportsmen involved, the Earl of March. He and the Earl of Eglintowne bet 1,000 guineas that four horses could pull a four-wheel chaise carrying one person nineteen miles in under an hour. They were taken up on it by Theobald Taafe and Andrew Sproule.

Previous page
The Chaise Match at
Newmarket
JAMES SEYMOUR

178

Seymour's painting shows the strange contrivance which was produced on the day to meet the wager. The four horses were all racers — three of them had won plates — and were ridden by jockeys. The boy passenger was placed precariously in the middle of the rear axle. He must have had an exhilarating experience, for contemporary accounts tell us that the horses were effectively out of control for the first four miles as the carriage bucketed along behind. However the riders eventually gained command, and comfortably covered the nineteen miles, with 6 minutes 33 seconds to spare.

This exotic contest clearly tickled the fancy of the English public, for engravings of Seymour's picture, and versions by other artists, were widely produced. Yet carriage racing, or trotting, was only occasionally to surface as a sport in England. The American trotter Tom Thumb came over to England and trotted a hundred miles on Sunbury Common, outside London, in 10 hours 7 minutes in 1829.

A century and a half later Prince Charles, the Prince of Wales, drove a trotter on the old Lanark racecourse in Scotland. But these excursions into publicity had little observable effect, and in these last years of the millennium trotting languishes where it has for centuries in Britain — still operating at a handful of modest venues, and cherished most by the gypsies and travelling folk who have steadfastly continued to nurture the trotting horse and the coloured horse amidst a nation devoted either to blood horses or its sturdy native breeds.

In America the earliest trot was recorded less fulsomely in print, and not at all, it seems, in oil on canvas. But it was to be the start of a much more magnificent tradition. The *New York Commercial Advertiser* of 11 June 1806 simply reported: 'A horse named Yankee trotted a mile yesterday in 2 minutes 59 seconds, in Harlem, New York.' From this first three-minute mile, trotting racing has largely been the story of contests against the clock. It is not the epic matches that loom in the sport's annals but the first horses to squeeze inside the constricting rigours of the stop watch. The first trotter to go a mile in under 2 minutes 30 seconds was Lady Suffolk pulling a wagon in 1845. She was the old grey mare of the song 'who ain't what she used to be' — scarcely surprising as she raced in seventeen states and usually had to get there under her own steam, pulling the wagon. The first trotter to go under 2 minutes 10 seconds was Maud S.; the first horse to go under two minutes was the pacer Star Pointer, followed in 1903 by the trotter Lou

Overleaf
Trotters Racing by the
Judge's Stand
LOUIS MAURER

179

Greyhound at Goshen RICHARD STONE REEVES

George M. Patchen, Brown Dick and Miller's Damsel
on the Union Course, 1859 LOUIS MAURER

Dillon. But perhaps the best loved trotter of all time was the grey gelding Greyhound. Richard Stone Reeves' painting shows him breaking two minutes for the mile — 1 minute 59¾ seconds — at Goshen in New York in 1937.

Historic Track, Goshen, in Orange County, is the headquarters of harness racing, a laurel bequeathed by generations of local enthusiasts who bred and raced many of America's best trotters and pacers. Goshen is a small neat dozing town sixty miles from Manhattan and light years away from the electronic frenzy of modern pacing at the

Meadowlands track. Yet Historic Track still maunders on at the back of Main Street, Goshen, tight up against the wooded hill, painted clapboard houses along the far bend and the blighted tree stump known as Hambletonian's oak in the centre of the track, glowering across at the stand. Alongside the old Club Room is Trotting Racing's Hall of Fame.

Greyhound has pride of place there, for in 1939, his sixth season, Greyhound trotted a mile in 1 minute 55¼ seconds at Lexington, Kentucky, a record which was to stand for more than thirty years, until Nevel Pride finally bettered it at Indianapolis in 1969. Greyhound trotted at tracks all over the United States; his coat, whitening year by year, became a talisman for harness racing fans at a time when the sport was hurt badly by the Depression. He even went down to Daytona Beach in Florida to see if he could better 1-50 on that level smooth sand. But Greyhound took against the ocean and the record never came.

There have, of course, been many great contests between trotters. There was a $500 purse at stake in the match which Louis Maurer painted in 1859 with George M. Patchen, Brown Dick and Miller's Damsel at the Union course. There were five one-mile heats and George M. Patchen took the money by winning three of them.

Today harness racing has spread worldwide, challenging and sometimes surpassing thoroughbred racing in popularity, not only in the United States and France, but also in Australia and many smaller countries. Even in England, a solitary sulky has been seen at dusk in recent years spinning across the thoroughbred turf of Newmarket, two and a half centuries after the famous chaise match of 1750 heralded a destiny yet to be fulfilled.

IX
Steeplechasing

Steeplechasing as an organised sport was not a decade old when William Tasker (1808–52) painted his study of the 1843 Grand National at Liverpool. The picture is an astonishing testament to the explosive growth of this novel attraction. The towering stand, four tiers high, had beggared the entrepreneur who had constructed it, the Liverpool publican William Lynn. But clearly if he had been able to stave off the men from Carey Street a little longer, he would have been a wealthy man. The tribunes are packed to the gills with intrepid enthusiasts, risking life and limb on the walls and cornices of the topmost layers. Alongside are the public dining rooms and the Towers Stand, in the background an array of beflagged tents and buildings catering to the needs of an enormous crowd.

There can have been few sporting ventures blessed with such immediate and enduring success as steeplechasing in England. The action on the course in Tasker's picture epitomises the attractions to the spectator of racing between the flags, which have scarcely changed in a century and a half since: daunting obstacles, shared courage of man and horse, thrills and spills. Modern painters shy a little from painting the spills, but the newspaper photographers focus unerringly to this day on the moments of disaster — even death — which have fascinated spectators ever since the first race at St Albans in 1831.

Tasker has painted the scene when Liverpool's terrifying wall was jumped for the last time. It was removed before the 1844 race. These days the water jump is in roughly the same position. The wall is fully twenty courses high, dwarfing the redcoat soldiers and spectators who stand beside it, a fearsome barrier which has already accounted for two of the runners, Teetotum and Tinderbox, who have both taken fearful falls and brought a builder's load of stones down behind them.

Lottery, the canny 1839 winner and his rider, dandy Jem Mason, are thankfully accepting an easy route through the rubble, before picking their way through the carnage on the other side. Tinderbox's jockey Moore suffered a broken collar bone. The eventual winner Vanguard, owned by Lord Chesterfield, is racing away. Out of the picture in front

Overleaf
Grand National 1843
WILLIAM TASKER

185

was the grey Peter Simple. He was destined to become the first of those famous Aintree characters, the gallant loser who never quite makes it. He was twice third and once second in five runnings. His ghost lives on in popular favourites like Wyndburgh and Greasepaint in modern times.

The madness for steeplechasing descended on the English sporting public quite suddenly in the 1830s. The annals of the old hunts in the previous hundred years are full of informal contests between the young thrusters in Leicestershire and Northamptonshire. Mr Farquharson, Hugo Meynell and Squire Osbaldeston are the names that live on from these races across country, with the finishing line flagged by some distant steeple. But the idea of racing round an organised course of obstacles in front of spectators had to wait until some cavalry officers and a publican staged the 1831 event at St Albans. The fever spread quickly. By the end of the decade there were huge crowds at Liverpool, Cheltenham and Nottingham for races that endure to this day. And there were instant heroes — horses like Lottery and riders like Jem Mason and Captain Machell.

The artists, swift in that era to serve a new market, turned with verve to subjects where there was so much colour, drama and comedy. Painters like Francis Calcraft Turner (1782–1846) and Henry Alken (1785–1851) and his family, who had enticed a large public to buy their portraits of the triumphs and pitfalls of the hunting field, now started to paint the steeplechasers.

The enchantment was lasting. A century and a half later artists like Peter Biegel (1913–87) and Michael Lyne (1912–89) could still produce their amused and atmospheric pictures, for steeplechasing has remained the glorious sport of romantic tales and racing for love, where an American amateur can win the Grand National and the Prince of Wales can end up on his bottom in the mud, and also where the toughest, bravest jockeys in the world risk their necks daily for a fraction of the rewards earned by the glamorous fraternity on the flat.

Henry Alken, who wrote under the pen name of Ben Tally Ho for the sporting press and signed some of his sketches thus, had gone to hunt in Leicestershire in the 1820s for sound journalistic reasons. The hunts were good copy, full of the undignified falls and upsets which appealed to Ben Tally Ho's readers. He must have blended in well 'with his broad-brimmed low crowned hat, his frock of Kendal green, spotted with broad gold

Opposite
Lottery and Valentine
FRANCIS CALCRAFT TURNER

188

Grand Leicestershire Steeplechase 1829 HENRY ALKEN. Charles Apperley (the writer 'Nimrod') is the starter, the famous huntsman Dick Christian is on the grey.

Christian has two falls and still finishes second. Mr Heycock falls off Clinker into a ditch. Mr Field Nicholson wins on Magic buttons — his rustic waistcoat with its low cut and old-fashioned pockets, his brown cloth kickseys, his ditto gaiters, his thick-soled shoes and sturdy walking staff,' as a friend described him in the *New Sporting Magazine*. 'The perfect inhabitant of those country scenes which he so skilfully depicts.' Indeed it was only after a considerable spell as a guest with the Melton Hunt and Sir Francis Burdett that Henry Alken spilled the beans during an extremely bibulous dinner party and revealed Ben Tally Ho's identity.

Any resentment at this subterfuge was seemingly drowned in the contents of the punch bowl, and Alken stayed on to become a close observer of the Leicestershire hunts. There are a number of pencil sketches and drawings of the Melton Hunt in 1826, and Alken was at hand to see the development from what could be called point to point racing, towards the formal racing over a precise course and fixed fences, usually specially constructed, which can be acknowledged as modern steeplechasing. In 1829 he was commissioned by a local Member of Parliament, Charles Hollingworth Magniac, to paint a set of eight pictures of the March steeplechase. These became, as prints, the most celebrated sporting series of the time before formal steeplechasing began.

In the Leicestershire steeplechase the riders are allowed to choose their own line for the four miles from Nowsley Wood to Billesdon Coplow. The intrepid figure on the grey who takes two tumbles and still almost wins is Dick Christian, whose memoirs are full of tales of this Leicestershire country — of a run to Billesdon Coplow when he jumped a tremendous fence on a wild grey and Sir Gilbert Heathcote's huntsman wouldn't follow. 'Sir Gilbert called, "You on a 400 guinea horse and you can't follow Dick. I'll discharge you if you don't." And discharge him he did.' Christian recalled half a dozen horses dying in the hunting field during one twenty-two mile run, so it was no surprise that quarter was scarce when it came to steeplechasing. The unfortunate figure flattened under his bay horse in the fifth picture is Mr Guilford. He was recorded as 'seriously hurt'. But the race went on to be won by Mr Field Nicholson on Magic.

For nearly all the early steeplechase artists, it was the daunting nature of the obstacles and the hideous falls which were the focus of attention. J. F. Herring in his carefully composed picture of steeplechase cracks in 1846, which featured Jem Mason on Lottery, Tom Oliver on Discount, and Allen McDonough on Brunette, chose to show the field jumping a stone wall. Though the Aintree wall had already been removed by this date,

Left
Jumping a Road
JOHN DALBY

Below
Steeplechase Cracks
JOHN FREDERICK HERRING

The St Albans Grand
Steeplechase 1834
JAMES POLLARD

the stone wall was to remain in place at other meetings and to provide a prime motif for the first generation of steeplechase artists. If a wall was not available, then another surprise sufficed, as in John Dalby's picture of two chasers crossing what is probably the Melling Road, a hazard which still exists at Aintree to this day, but is buried annually in bark to save the horses' feet.

James Pollard's bright and vivacious picture of the 1834 St Albans steeplechase shows clearly how the sport had evolved from the cross-country racing of the hunting bloods. This was primarily the work of Thomas Coleman, the landlord of the Turf Hotel at St Albans. Coleman had been an astute trainer of flat race horses at Brocket Hall, then, as now, an immaculate and enviable stretch of parkland near St Albans. But his talents extended to a flair for innovation and publicity. He had rebuilt the Turf on the site of the old Chequers Hotel and installed baths which were a tourist attraction in themselves, for they enjoyed the exquisite luxury of hot and cold water. He attracted the roistering set who dominated racing in those days: John Gully, the prizefighter turned bookmaker; Lord George Bentinck, at once gambler and Turf reformer; and Squire Osbaldeston, the greatest sportsman of the day who lost, he claimed, £3,000 in a night in Coleman's new billiard room.

It was in this red-blooded milieu, and, the story has it, after a dinner held by officers from the Life Guards, that Coleman elaborated his scheme to enhance the appeal of his hostelry — and, as it transpired, lay claim to found the true sport of steeplechasing. Coleman's idea was to publish conditions for the race as in flat racing — it was 11 stone 7 pounds over four miles in 1831 — to have a properly marked course with flags, and to have the winner sold for £500. It was to be a contest for spectators — his customers — and not just for the joy of the riders. Coleman at first kept the course secret and hid his flag men in ditches until the last moment, but this experiment quickly died. Pollard's lively painting shows just how well Coleman's venture succeeded. Here, at the finish, there is a respectably-sized crowd, corralled by cords. Most have come on foot, but there are coaches and small carriages, with a handsome bell tent, presumably for the convenience of either judges or spectators. A number of mounted enthusiasts are dashing along on the far side, having followed the action further down the course. Pollard has given us a tight finish to round off an exhilarating March scene.

The Paddock at Cheltenham LIONEL EDWARDS

1934 Grand National
CHARLES SIMPSON

James Pollard is most noted for his coaching pictures which were finely executed with great precision, and are indeed an authoritative record of that brief half century when the coaches ruled the new turnpikes, and the railways had not yet arrived to consign them to Christmas cards and memories. Born in London, the son of a painter, Pollard also painted many racing scenes and collaborated with other notable artists like Herring, before his wife and daughter both died in 1840 and the verve went out of his work as well as his life.

By 1838 the St Albans steeplechase was in decline, but Coleman's idea had spawned thirty-nine meetings at locations all over England that year and launched a sport which in its apogee, the Aintree Grand National, probably attracts more interest than any other race in the world.

Aintree and Cheltenham were to emerge as the two premier courses of English steeplechasing, though for almost a century until the rise of the Gold Cup at Cheltenham in the 1920s Aintree was unchallenged as the supreme test of the chasing horse. Both courses have become associated with heroic horses, from Lottery in the first Nationals to Red Rum in the 1970s, and from Golden Miller to Dawn Run at Cheltenham.

J. F. Herring painted Lottery with Jem Mason in the saddle, but the nineteenth-century heroes of steeplechasing were ill served by artists, who seem to have deemed the thrills and spills of the sport to be more commercial than adulation of its champions. The result is a palpably strip-cartoon quality to much of the painting of Victorian chasing scenes. By contrast, many of the outstanding equestrian painters of the twentieth century, from Gilbert Holiday to Michael Lyne, have shown a great affinity for steeplechasing. And some of the great chasers received their due on canvas.

Charles Simpson's (1885–1971) picture of the 1934 Grand National is a fine action study of two superb horses in one of the golden eras of steeplechasing. The leading horse is Golden Miller, perhaps the greatest steeplechaser ever to have run in England. He won five consecutive Cheltenham Gold Cups at a time when there were the most worthy of opponents, Thomond II, Kellsboro' Jack and Forbra, to challenge him.

Golden Miller, obscurely bred by a five-guinea-a-time sire, Goldcourt, out of a mare called Miller's Pride, was nevertheless big and handsome enough to make 1,000 guineas as a yearling at Ballsbridge sales in Ireland. He eventually ended, for a dozen times that sum, in the hands of the young Dorothy Paget. Miss Paget, reclusive, eccentric, and by

Opposite
Canal Turn MICHAEL LYNE

A Big Field
PETER BIEGEL

all accounts a spectacular gambler, was a familiar portly figure on the racecourse, invariably dressed in a blue hat and a blue tent-like coat which stretched towards her ankles. She was not known for her loyalty to jockeys or trainers. Golden Miller had seventeen different riders in the course of his career, and between them they managed twenty-nine victories.

Simpson's picture, of the final stages of the race, shows Golden Miller in his *annus mirabilis*, when he won both the Gold Cup and the Grand National. His victory in the 1934 National, carrying over 12 stone yet knocking eight seconds off the course record, was one of the most memorable duels of that celebrated decade. For most of the race, Golden Miller was racing alongside the previous winners Forbra and Gregalach with two other great horses who were destined never to win the race, Thomond II and Really True. But it was the nine-year-old Delaneige who hung on to jump the last almost alongside Golden Miller. Charles Simpson's painting, as though gazing upwards, has caught both the horses in a majestic leap, both jockeys poised and concentrating. In the final run Delaneige was to be left five lengths behind.

Simpson, who had been attached to the Newlyn School of painters in Cornwall, only turned to equestrian painting in middle life after he had become involved in a rodeo which came to Wembley in London. Though some of his portraits can be unexciting, there are few better tributes to a great steeplechaser than this memorial of Golden Miller's finest moment, winning over the course he clearly hated most, and which was to bring him to grief twice in two days the following year when his connections insanely ran him in the Champion Chase after he had fallen at the Canal Turn in the National.

Kellsboro' Jack, the subject of Lynwood Palmer's (1861–1941) painting was the Grand National winner of 1933. Year by year through to the present day the National has thrown up romantic tales, from Moifaa the New Zealand horse who swam away from a shipwreck and survived to run in the 1904 National and win, up to Little Polvier who was sold to a young soldier in 1989 as 'past his racing best' and came back to victory at Aintree.

Kellsboro' Jack finished amongst the also-rans behind Golden Miller in the 1933 Cheltenham Gold Cup. His owner, the American businessman and art collector F. Ambrose Clark, had sold him despairingly to his wife Florence for £1 in an effort to

Opposite
Kellsboro' Jack
LYNWOOD PALMER

Becher's LIONEL EDWARDS

change the horse's luck. Mr Clark himself ran the ten-year-old Chadd's Ford in the National. Kellsboro' Jack was just seven years old and was given only a 25/1 chance by the bookmakers at Aintree, as not only Golden Miller but also Gregalach, Remus, and Delaneige were in the field. The pace was fast and Golden Miller was going well until the public were aghast to see their invincible favourite unseat his rider at the Canal Turn, the second time around. Kellsboro' Jack and Pelorus Jack were left in front, matching strides until the final fence when Pelorus fell. Kellsboro' Jack was left to win as he pleased. Florence Clark immediately announced that he would be rewarded by being excused the Aintree fences forever. Ambrose Clark rewarded himself by commissioning Lynwood Palmer's painting, in which he appears with the horse and with Ivor Anthony, his trainer, at Wroughton in Wiltshire. Kellsboro' Jack's National jockey Dudley Williams wears the winning silks. Mrs Clark is absent.

Lynwood Palmer, an Englishman who had taken up painting in America, had returned home at the turn of the century and found great popularity among some of the most discriminating patrons of the day. There is a suffused, muted quality to this study of Kellsboro' Jack, as there is to many of the pictures he painted for the Duke of Portland and King Edward VII. He made great efforts to get to know a horse before he painted it, prizing an ability to capture its individuality and personality, which was endorsed by the loyalty of his patrons.

X
This Day and Age

Racing art today is a truly popular art form, reflecting the huge appeal which the sport now holds not just for the enthusiastic racegoer but for the millions who watch it on television, and the high stakes that are now brought into play. Céleste Susany's picture of the Breeders' Cup Classic in 1987 shows one of the rare occasions in American racing when the champion of one generation takes on the champion of the year before. Three million dollars in prize money for one race makes even the allure of a season's stud fees pall. Owners of colts can easily be persuaded to keep them in training and abjure the attractions of despatching them early to stallion duties if they can aspire to such an enormous pot of gold at the end of the season.

The November afternoon light was already fading when Ferdinand and Alysheba went to the start for the 1987 Classic at Hollywood Park, California. Ferdinand was the 1986 Kentucky Derby winner. His jockey Bill Shoemaker, the all-time American champion, had had to steer him like a stock car through the field before he just touched off the English colt Bold Arrangement at the line. A year later Alysheba had won the 1987 Derby in almost effortless fashion, with Chris McCarron riding. As they came left-handed in to the final turn at Hollywood Park, the two Derby winners had left the rest of the field lost in the gloom. Throughout the length of the final stretch, the race was run as true as perfection could demand. Alysheba, athletic and exuberant, came with what seemed to be a decisive turn of speed. Ferdinand, tough and mature, never flinched. The Hollywood Park crowd, often cynically accustomed to regarding horses as mere numbers, erupted in a prolonged roar as Ferdinand held on to win by a short head.

Paintings of such encounters, and especially the fine prints which are distributed in limited editions, are as eagerly sought today as Henry Alken and Harry Hall's aquatints were tracked down a century or more ago. The exploits and portraits of John Henry, Cozzene, and the Derby-winning filly Winning Colors appear now not only in oils and prints, but on scarves and porcelain plates and table mats, just as they did in nineteenth-century England.

Alysheba and Ferdinand CELESTE SUSANY

Trainer's View DAVID PAVLAK

The association of art with racing, deeper and more enduring, it seems, than with any other sport, is founded now, as then, on the acute emotions which racehorses arouse. For racing is not merely about victory and defeat, heroes and heroines, stars and bit-part players. There is an aesthetic appeal about the blood horse, the skein of muscle and power, the explosive speed, the mystical grace of horses working in the early morning, the languid routines of summer stables, which nourishes a romantic appreciation exemplified by modern equestrian painters.

The New York painter Anthony M. Alonso, who has often painted the paddocks, the

Starter's View DAVID PAVLAK

Cozzene — Turning for Home ANTHONY M. ALONSO

Easy Goer – Break to Glory ANTHONY M. ALONSO

Looking Back JAMES L. CROW

backstretch and the workaday routines of the track, says that he sets out to tantalise the eye and orchestrate the emotions of the viewer. 'The romance is putting in the atmosphere, the horse and its environment.' The misty play of light in James L. Crow's seductive paintings, though unsentimental, is unashamedly romantic too. *Looking Back* is a precise rendering of a familiar moment on the track as the challengers start to range up behind the leader. Yet the subtle colours, the neutral background, the legendary head of the horse and the ethereal play of light on its quarters all coalesce in a work of undisguised emotionalism.

Many contemporary painters have placed the artist and the viewer as a participant in the action on the canvas. David Pavlak's vertiginous view from the trainer's seat, behind

In the Bunch CHRISTINE PICAVET

a black trotter on a snowy track, with the white wheel lines careering past and out of sight, is a whirlwind of a picture. His painting *The Starter's View* portrays those tense moments when the pacers seem destined to drive in to the starting gate before the starter's car surges away to liberate them on to the open track. The traditions, too, of the cinema — surprising angles, uncompromising close-ups — also permeate modern racing painting. The contemporary eye, educated to the patterns of the telephoto lens, accepts the isolation of the close-up and the exaggerations of carefully lit and highlighted features, muscles and rippling skin. Christine Picavet's studies at the California tracks have just such a cinematic feel and focus.

Racing art, essentially realistic in style yet romantic in inspiration, has diverged far these days from the centre stream of modernist art. Scenes lively enough to attract Manet, Degas, or Toulouse-Lautrec hold scant appeal for the artists of the late twentieth century. A few, like Skeaping and, in America, Fay Moore, have brought some of the conventions and devices of modern painting to the racetrack. Yet the best of sporting painting through the centuries has sprung from a sure foundation in the knowledgeable and discriminating eye of horsemen and women, whose deep attachment to the thoroughbred horse and his epic deeds has also been inspirational.

The discernment of quality has always been essential to their business and their pleasure, and this rigour has applied to the art they patronise. The best, to this day, is fine and unsentimental, yet suffused with passionate enthusiasm, and it is fair to predict that it will prove as enduring as the work of those masters who, for nearly three hundred years, have led the way.

216

Last Furlong JOHN SKEAPING

Acknowledgements

The pictures in this book come from four continents. Only unstinting help from old friends and from strangers who have become friends, from the knowledgeable officers of public collections across the world, and from the private collectors who have allowed me to reproduce so many of their pictures, have together made this publication possible. They all have my heartfelt thanks.

In particular I would like to acknowledge the help of Phil Pines and Gail Cunard at the Hall of Fame of the Trotter at Goshen, New York; of Kathryn Schrade at the National Museum of Racing at Saratoga, New York; and of Claudia Briggs and Deborah Keaveney at Christie's in London. Marilyn Hunt at the Yale Center for British Art and Beverly Carter at the Mellon Collection gave their usual swift and expert help in the United States, as did David Fuller at Ackermann's and Richard Green in London. Gloria Harris at Christie, Manson and Woods in New York and Mary Moore Jacoby at the Virginia Museum tracked down elusive pictures for me. Didi Marks at the York Racing Museum, Juliet Johnson at Frost and Reed and Julia Stone at the William Marler Gallery gave me special help, as did Rita Robbins at Wildenstein and Co in New York and Captain John Macdonald-Buchanan. At John Murray I have had the blessing of an enthusiastic and creative editor, Ariane Goodman, and a talented art director, Beverley Waldron.

Individual pictures which can be acknowledged are listed below. All other pictures were either lent by the artist, or by collectors who wish to remain anonymous.

Her Majesty the Queen and her Horse Aureole by Sir Alfred Munnings is reproduced by gracious permission of Her Majesty the Queen.
Steeplechase Cracks and *Cotherstone and his Forebears*, both by John Frederick Herring, are reproduced by gracious permission of Her Majesty Queen Elizabeth the Queen Mother.

I should also like to thank:
Allison Galleries, New York, for *The Sealskin Brigade* by Nicholas Winfield Scott Leighton.
Arthur Ackermann and Son for *Isinglass* by G. D. Giles; *Prince George's Leedes* by John Wootton; *Starling at Newmarket* by Thomas Spencer; *Whisker Beating Raphael* by John Nost Sartorius; *Start at Newmarket* by John Wootton; *Becher's* by Lionel Edwards; *Weighing Room* by Peter Biegel; *Last Furlong* and *The Race* by John Skeaping; *Lester Piggott* by Raymond Skipp.

Fool by Richard Stone Reeves; *Secretariat* by John Skeaping; *The United States Hotel,* unattributed; *The First Futurity* by Louis Maurer; *Oklahoma* by Elmore Brown.

National Trust for Scotland for *The 1844 Derby* by John Frederick Herring.

National Trust for Scotland, Brodick Castle for *The St Albans Grand Steeplechase* by James Pollard.

The Paul Mellon Collection for *Settling Day at Tattersalls* by James Pollard; *The Chaise Match* by James Seymour.

The Racquet and Tennis Club of New York for *Kellsboro' Jack* by Lynwood Palmer.

Red Fox Fine Art, Middleburg, Virginia for *Canal Turn* by Michael Lyne.

Richard Green (Fine Paintings) for *Newmarket Heath with Horses Exercising* by James Seymour; *Racehorse Galloping with Jockey Up* by Charles Towne; *John Gully's Colt Pyrrhus the First* by John Frederick Herring; *John Gully's Filly Mendicant* by John Frederick Herring; *The Paddock at Cheltenham* by Lionel Edwards.

Royal Academy of Art, London/Bridgeman Art Library, London for drawing from *The Anatomy of the Horse* by George Stubbs.

Royal Borough of Kingston upon Thames for photographs by Eadweard Muybridge.

Royal Hong Kong Jockey Club for *Night Racing at Happy Valley* by Roy Miller.

Sir Alfred Munnings Art Museum, Dedham, Essex for *Study of Jockeys and Horses* and *Under Starter's Orders, Newmarket*.

Sir Nicholas Lyell QC, MP for *Racing* and *Steeplechase* by Lowes Dalbiac Luard.

Sotheby's, New York for *The Paddock* by Raoul Dufy; *Merman* by Emil Adam; *Longchamp* by Peter le Bihan; *Match Between the Barry and the Meynell Hounds* by Francis Sartorius; *General Chasse* by John Ferneley; *La Toucques* by Harry Hall.

Stadt Essen Museum for *Riders on the Beach* by Paul Gauguin.

Tate Gallery, London for *A Jockeys' Changing Room* by Sir John Lavery; Tate Gallery/Bridgeman Art Library, London for *Derby Day* by William Powell Frith and *Mares and Foals* by George Stubbs.

Tryon Gallery, London for *1934 Grand National* by Charles Simpson.

Victoria and Albert Museum, London for *The Betting Post* by Thomas Rowlandson; Victoria and Albert/Bridgeman Art Library, London for *The Road to Epsom* by Thomas Rowlandson.

Virginia Museum of Fine Arts, Richmond for *Blue Grass Races* by Kees van Dongen; *Return from the Race* by Alfred de Dreux; *Trotting at the Union Raceway* by Henri DeLattre; *A Ladies' Horse Race* by Thomas Nicholson; *Horseback Riding, Chantilly* by Jacques Villon; *The Races* by Pierre Bonnard; *Deauville Races* by Jean Louis Forain; *Ascot* by Raoul Dufy.

Walker Art Gallery, Liverpool for *Lottery and Valentine* by Francis Calcraft Turner; *Jumping a Road* by John Dalby.

Walters Art Gallery, Baltimore for *Race of the Riderless Horses in Rome* by Theodore Géricault.

William Marler Gallery, Cirencester for *Tattenham Corner* and *Rainbow Start* by Gilbert Holiday.

Yale Center for British Art, New Haven, Connecticut for *Grand National 1843* by William Tasker.

York Racing Museum for *Alicia Thornton's Match Against Captain Flint*.

Index